CW01594500

TRIUMPH HOUSE
Poetry with a Purpose

A PICTURE OF RHYME

Edited by

Tim Christian

First published in Great Britain in 2001 by
TRIUMPH HOUSE
Remus House,
Coltsfoot Drive,
Peterborough, PE2 9JX
Telephone (01733) 898102

HB ISBN 1 86161 844 1
SB ISBN 1 86161 849 2

FOREWORD

In today's modern world everyone's life is fast-moving and hectic, leaving little time to stop, open our minds and gather together our thoughts. However, there are times when we really do need to take time out to sort our feelings and emotions. Poetry can very often provide us with much-needed release by allowing us to express and share our important thoughts with others.

A Picture Of Rhyme is a special collection of these poems, featuring the work of over 150 new and established authors of today.

Together they combine their creative talents to present to you an inspiring and enjoyable read that you will want to return to time and time again.

Tim Christian
Editor

Contents

The Poet Laurie Utt	Stephen Dipré	1
Little Horror	Jennie Rippon	2
Why?	Maggie Moore	3
Insurrection	Peter Davies	4
The Generation Gap	Cecil J Lewis	5
Widow's Song	Lynne Griffiths	6
All That Glitters	Raymond K Evans	6
The Other Queen Of Scots	Bob Jenkins	7
A Secret Place	Flora Denning	7
Broken-Hearted	Isla Isbister	8
Two-Faced January	Helen M Seeley	8
Pop Concert	Winifred Thorpe	9
Forest Homes	Shirley H Ford	10
Rhyme	Danny Coleman	10
A Man I Know	Sally Warren	11
Winter	T P Bradley	11
The View From The Hill	Peter W P Turner	12
Can Believe	Hugh Campbell	13
I Little Thought	Robert D Hayward	14
My Hero	Sonia Mills	15
I Am Love	Jennifer Stella Smeed	16
My Cat Has Lost His Miaow	Eileen Sugden	17
Meg	Iaian W Wade	18
Class And Breeding	John J Hudson	19
My Sweet Diamond Ring	Joyce Hemsley	20
Wishing	Janet Fish	20
Man's Journey	Terry Daley	21
Faces	Josephine Pollacco	22
Mourning Anger	Douglas Bishop	23
Incomprehension	Catherine May	24
Inside Story	Jocelyn McKinnon	25
Beyond Belief	Lisa Harrison	26
Pacemaker	Mollie Catlin	27
The Vale Of Tears	Margi Hughes	28
True Friends	G Whitten	29
The Wings Of Autumn	Sheila Pharo	30

Starry Night	June Prescott	30
The New Allotment	Barbara Delaney	31
Ye Olde Curiosity Shop	Bernice Sharpe	32
A Pig's Life	Gordon Knight	33
We Talk Of Love Quite Often	Jeanette Gaffney	34
I Want To Be An AA Man	Jane Phillimore	35
Dreaming!	James Ellis	36
The Salvation Army Band	Freda Lily Lawrence	36
Cooking For Christmas	Perry McDaid	37
Joys Of The King's Head Inn	Rosemary Remy	38
Arrogatus	Jeanette Smith	39
Ginger Tom Cat	Lucy Porter	40
The Holiday Home	A E Doney	41
Snooker, Of Course!	Frank Parker	42
All Hallows Eve	Kathleen Mary Scatchard	42
The Cold Face Of Winter	Iris Taylor	43
Leaves And Broken Branches	M Burleigh	44
The Greatest Love	Una Allan	44
My Backyard	Judith Thomas	45
We Are All Equal	Penny Bunce	46
Pheasant Wedding Spree	Françoise de Pierpont	47
One Word	M A Honeyman	48
Splish! Splash! Splosh!	Betty E Keeler	49
Hope Springs . . .	Jenny Proom	50
A Mountain Stroll	Idwal B Holt	51
One Day I Looked For Her	Christine Saunders	52
With Thanks	Joy Townsley	52
When Winter Comes	J M Drinkhill	53
A Time For Rhyme	Betty Green	54
Felix	Geraldine Page	55
Nirvana	Anita Richards	56
I Wish I Had A Mummy And Daddy	Don Woods	57
Rubbish	Yvonne Burgess	58
Autumn	Marie Stewart	58
Fear	C A Jones	59
Who Wants To Be A Millionaire?	Patricia Anne Turner	60

Contemplation And Observation	Catherine Buchan	61
Steam Days	Bobbie Dee	62
Mr Moon	Sue Cox	62
In Praise Of The Dome	Susan Holmquist	63
Aspects Of Love	I Lott	64
Thanks From A Stranger	Norman Chandler	65
Ode To Booze	Derek J Morgan	66
Happiness	Glenis Dando	66
Autumn	Linda Daly	67
The Frost Bird	Ancilla Dent	67
Old Man	Karen McBean	68
Volcano's Threat	J Naylor	69
Book Of Dreams	Bakewell Burt	70
Beware	D J Tucker	70
Careless	Ann Copland	71
Wee 'Bon'	Julie D Coventry	72
Blue Moon	Richard J Godwin	72
Prelude To Summertime	Kay House	73
The Dream	Marie Wilson	74
Time's Up	Joan Burdon	75
God Is Every Poem I Write	Mary Seddon	76
Poetry	A T Giddings	77
Hallowe'en	Fine Buliciri	78
Cat-Thief	Julia Middleton	79
Ticking Away	Kate Stobart	80
A Walk On The Moors Above Haworth	Ellie Lomas	81
Fat Cat	Bridget Drinkwater	82
The Dream Catcher	Sally Bush	82
The Cure	Patricia Farley	83
Burning Passion	Rosemary Cook	84
Retired	Eileen Cuddy-Buckley	85
Tell Me Why?	N Young	86
The Nail-Scarred Invitation	Ian Caughey	87
Crunch Time	Steven Millhouse	88
Over My Dead Body	Nita Garlinge	89
Residuum	Louise Rogers	90

A Verse Too Far	E J Nickson	90
My Quiet Place	Marion Pollitt	91
You	Colin Farquhar	91
Behind The Scene	T A Napper	92
Loss	Betty M Varley	92
The Ghost Of Dreams	Pat Fortune	93
Ode To Black Beauty	Doreen E Roberts	94
River Spey	Alister H Thomson	95
Five-Fifteen	Marc Tyler	96
A Stay In Hospital	Sue Vince	96
Rhyme Is Yours And Mine	A J Ferguson	97
Jason	Christina Carville	98
Old Faithful	Bill Williamson	98
Meg	Rebecca Punter	99
Abortion	Mary Hoey	100
Foetus	L K Clements	101
Time For Rhyme	Stanley Swann	102
Pebbles On A Beach	R Humphrey	102
If I Have To Wait	Linda Brown	103
Abandonment	J F Grainger	104
Beddgelert	Christopher Higgins	105
The Steam Train	Pauletta Edwards	106
A Judge	Fatty R	107
The Shire Horse Courage	Wendy Watkin	108
The Clock	Phil Robinson	109
Rose Of Beauty	Susan Amphlett	110
To Rhyme Or Not To Rhyme	Pauline Anderson	110
Song Of Happiness	Violet M Corlett	111
Seashore Shells	Terry Daley	112
Praise Your Maker	Anthony Gibson	113
First Winter	Nicola Staniland	114
Sebastian	Lyndsey Louise Watson	115
Autumn Journey	Molly Rodgers	115
The Choir	Nina Havers	116
Messages	P Ludgate	116
The Sea Loch	Colin Wright	117
Trains Get My Vote	Tina Lipman	118
Question	Marnie Connley	119

Just Another Day	Janice L Williams	120
Beneath The Desert Sun	Peter Hicks	121
Leo The Lion	Christopher Head	122
Reincarnation	Helen Persse	122
Friendship	Mary Antcliffe	123
Life Today	S A Clough	124
Froggy!	Graham Mitchell	124
To Elizabeth On The Loss Of Her Pony	Jane Finlayson	125
My Garden Gay	Richard Styles	126
Country Concerto	K G Johnson	127
Babies	Julie Sennitt	128

The Poet Laurie Utt

Laurie writes for a family readership
Never serves up any smut
Safely study him with Mother
The Poet Laurie Utt

He's tackled a huge range of subjects
From vintage cars to mud huts
Please enjoy him at your leisure
The Poet Laurie Utt

Insists on working in private
His study door's always shut
Don't dare break his concentration
The Poet Laurie Utt

He's got an instinct for what he likes
Can feel it in his guts
If it's not up to scratch he'll bin it
The Poet Laurie Utt

Laurie's always been prolific
Never been in a writer's block rut
If he dries up he'll retire
The Poet Laurie Utt

To some he's a poetic hero
To others he's simply nuts
Love him or loathe him
The Poet Laurie Utt

Dismisses all claims to greatness
Doesn't crave praise but
I am sure he'd love it if crowned
The next Poet Laureate

Stephen Dipré

Little Horror

I'm a lovely little girl and my name is Mary Jane
My mother and my father tell me I can be a pain.

I really look like butter would not melt in my mouth.
And yet I did some dreadful things when we lived in the south.

I put ants in grandma's teacup which she thought were dregs of tea.
She drank it down and smiled and was very nice to me.

I put superglue on Grandpa's chair and then when he sat down.
His pants stuck to the chair and he did much more than frown.

My bottom was quite sore that day, my pocket money stopped.
I screamed blue murder all the time as up and down I hopped.

But still that didn't cure me of doing naughty things.
I went to Mother's bedroom and hid all of her rings.

And Father didn't get away scot-free, without a doubt.
I spread word through the village that he was a lager lout.

I said he'd smashed our greenhouse whilst somewhat worse for wear.
And Mrs Brown is now convinced he can't be trusted anywhere.

When Aunty Sylvie came to stay I put worms in her bed.
She screamed so much and carried on I thought she'd end up dead.

I really thought she'd kill me. Why do I always get the blame?
I wore my little innocent look, but I got punished all the same.

I don't think they believed that it was really Jack, our dog.
Especially since he died last year from falling off a log.

I wish I had a sister whose pigtails I could pull
Or shut her in the field with Farmer Johnson's fierce new bull.

I really am a horror - I know that they are right
Yet I still dream up more mischief when I go to bed each night.

I don't think I can cure myself but they've promised me a pup
If I'll stop playing pranks and act a little bit grown up.

Jennie Rippon

WHY?

Observers watched the planet Earth, to see had it progressed,
And to see if *Man's* intelligence has passed their simple test.
Just to fill the world with peace and love, to extend a helping hand
To anything less fortunate, whether sea-bound or on land.

But what they saw enraged them, the Earth was split in two,
It seemed only to be ruled by what you could, or could not do.
On the one hand it was opulent, milk and honey there was plenty,
On the other hand was poverty, every grain store sadly empty.

Then there were the animals, and the creatures of the sea,
Didn't they deserve compassion and some humanity?
But their seas were being polluted, their jungles built upon,
Some were hounded to extinction, no one cared when they were gone!

Not content with the destruction being wrought upon the Earth,
Man now turned upon each other, as each seemed of little worth.
Country battled country for what little there was left,
Not caring who got in the way, or who was left bereft.

Since *Man* evolved and was allowed to shape his destiny,
He's filled his world with greed and hate, and bloody tyranny.
The observer then decided that the Earth just had to die,
And, as it spun into oblivion, *Man* looked up and shouted *'Why?'*

Maggie Moore

INSURRECTION

As eyelids droop, as senses fade,
Grim Reaper come and wield your blade,
And go your ways, bewildered clan,
And mourn her passing if you can.

If you imbibe what teachers teach,
If you believe what preachers preach,
Find solace for your troubled breast,
'Safe in the arms of Jesus' rest.

But if with restless, stubborn streak
Blind retribution you would seek,
For hawk that masquerades as dove
For cruel, unrequited love.

In humbleness we understand,
Come walk again across the land,
Go shed a tear for Blackwood mean,
Go dream again at Gwynfa green.

Demand to be the blushing bride
Whom siblings, spouse and son denied,
Strike out at blitz and scrimp and scrape,
At childbirth, squalor, war and rape.

They promised this, they promised that,
Not damp and draughty attic flat,
Go shake your fist and rant and rave
At unresponsive granite grave.

Now Mother mine, the die is cast,
Return from whence you came at last,
No longer held by bond nor creed,
A soul at peace, a spirit freed.

Peter Davies

The Generation Gap

Acknowledging the difference
Dividing age from youth
Yet surely sometimes seeking
The same eternal truth?

We look at life together
Though often seem to see
With differing perspective
And act accordingly.

Facing the same problems
On impulse youth may act
While we may think experience
Calls for a little tact.

Despite the disappointments
And burdens we both bear
A vision of the future
We elders also share.

Though youth with all the answers
May find our ways too slow
In spite of our experience
How little we all know.

While youth must learn its lessons
And conquer its heartaches
We elders must be patient
Remembering our mistakes.

Although a timeless problem
Seeking the same end
A vision of the future
Youth and experience blend.

Cecil J Lewis

WIDOW'S SONG

My days are long and lonely
without you by my side;
and it is only my pillows
that know of the tears I've cried.

The Lord saw fit to call you
and leave me here, behind.
Now I must carry on,
although strength is hard to find.

I long for time to come
when the Lord will call me too;
And when He does, my love,
I'll be coming straight to you.

I am yearning for the time
when I'll be back by your side,
but until that time comes
I'll remember you with pride.

Lynne Griffiths

ALL THAT GLITTERS

Money! Money is the 'Pied Piper' of Avarice,
jangling its tune in your pocket.
It strokes the ego of the shallow-minded.
Can control, bedazzle, till you're totally blinded.
Money! You rustle up dreams of possessions untold.
But, you have no heart! You have no soul!
So, take heed my friend! Set your sights on other goals.
For there are jewels to be had, much more precious than gold.

Raymond K Evans

THE OTHER QUEEN OF SCOTS

We are sorry to report in this sombre verse
That Gillian is leaving (our Scottish nurse)
She's ambitious and keen to try things new
But will miss the Ongar District Nurse Crew

This leaves Margo and the dedicated staff
Caring and supporting with the occasional laugh
Looking after the sick, disabled and blind
Doing their duties with a clear and sharp mind

So it's farewell to Gillian as she leaves Banson's Lane
Away from the needles, the dressings and the pain
Studying and working to achieve and attain
But 'Will ye no come back again?'

Bob Jenkins

A SECRET PLACE

I know of a secret place.
Where sunbeams dance across my face
Through leafy trees, where bluebells grow
And wood anemones, like drifts of snow.

A place that's quiet and so serene
Where I can sit and dream and dream.
The wood pigeon's there and the blue barred jay
And I can while my time away.

Clear water tumbles in the shallow brook,
The raucous voice of the widowed weeds rook.
I know of a secret place
Where sunbeams dance across my face.

Flora Denning

Broken-Hearted

I am stuck in the middle, like a pillar or post,
between the two people in this world I love most.
They say nasty words about each other to me,
I wish and I wish, they would just let me be.

I hate it, I hate it, and I break down and cry.
Sometimes I feel I could curl up and die.
But what can I do? Nothing at all.
It makes me so angry all the arguing they do.
I feel sad and upset and lonely too.

My smile has gone, faded away.
Maybe somehow it shall return someday.
All the happiness is lost that I had inside,
each day I wish I could confide.

The hurt inside, it always gets more,
with all this sadness, my heart has tore.
One day I hope it will all end, so my dreams can be fulfilled
and my love and heart once again I can built.

Isla Isbister

Two-Faced January

Days that are a dull drab grey
That gloat over autumn's debris dead
When there's no hint of summer's day
Beneath unbroken skies of lead.

Days that are a pure delight,
A foretaste, a reminder of spring
When the world half wakes in the sunlight
And the winter birds excitedly sing.

Helen M Seeley

Pop Concert

I stood in the crowd clapping and singing,
Hottest pop star in my ears his song ringing.
There were thousand of us
With our dreadlocks and ringlets,
With holes in our pants,
We all stood there singing.

I, waving my arms in the air while I sway,
Closing my eyes to the beat, enjoying my day.

The pop star looked down, picks me out of the crowd,
And gives me a smile and a wink.
His hair is red and he stands out a mile,
I feel my legs start to sink.

It's time to go home after such a long day,
I look at the others
They're young, they can stay.

I made my way back on a bus and a train,
Maybe next year I'll do it again.

When I got back the lock's on the door,
Matron please let me in.
I'm back from my trip, I know it's past ten,
I promise, I won't stay out again.

At my age it's silly, I'm now 82
But just for a while I felt quite new.

They let me in and I fell on the bed,
With the pop star's song ringing in my head.
What a wonderful day I feel I have lived,
Like when I was young just for a while,
I sleep, and my face holds a smile.

Winifred Thorpe

Forest Homes

The kitchen was the hub of home, of life it was the pivot.
The fire was always in the grate, the kettle on the trivet.
Its doors rang out with laughter and now and then with strife.
Sometimes it witnessed sorrow, the grief and pain of life.
Its walls absorbed the atmosphere and held all precious memories dear.

The parlour was a sacred place, used on very special days,
And though the houses were quite small, was hardly ever used at all.
There always was a sideboard, a polished table, too,
Several family photographs, a silver cup on view.
It was the family room of state - its atmosphere inanimate.

Shirley H Ford

Rhyme

My favourite form of communication,
rhyme is unexpectedly exciting.
It can be appreciated by a nation,
of readers in love with writing.
Paragraphs, pages of rhyme to move and stir,
kindle emotions which have begun to blur.
With weighty, soul testing, everyday living,
another day, week, year, unforgiving.
Will we pass the test, and finally retire,
when older, will our hearts still burn fire?
It is possible to still be passionate, create
when we are past, our sell by date?
I don't know, sometime I don't care.
I just think it would be easier,
with someone there to share.

Danny Coleman

A Man I Know

I met him at the fair many years ago,
A friendship began and I have come to know,
A man you can trust, like no one else before
We have spent all those years together and I hope forever more.
It is he that picks me up when I feel blue
And the only man who has been so true.
I will care for him always, we will never part,
He is special to me and belongs inside my heart.
This man is my husband and without a lie,
There is no way on earth I could ever say goodbye,
He's given me so much when life has let me down,
He's there for me when no one else is around.
If I ever lost him, life would never be the same,
So for now and forever, together we will remain.

Sally Warren

Winter

Now that dawn slumbers, slow to rise
And golden leaves glisten, jewelled by night's rain
And fallen, they waltz to winter's wind
As bristling bushes meet morning again.

How distant the memories of hazy days
When even the winds were warm
And sun slept little from scarlet set
To another bright diamond dawn.

But soon a new cold air will toil
Crisping a crust to slumbering soil
And herald spring's bulbs, and on dark stark trees,
A fresh green glimpse of brave new leaves.

T P Bradley

The View From The Hill

Time! To unlock the soul,
Release the words . . . hidden within.
To let, the ball pen roll . . .
To tap the keys . . .
Write, that poetry, to gladden,
To enthral, to please
Ones weary, heavy heart.

I have let the ink flow . . .
Like the River Cuckmere
Peacefully, meandering below,
As from up above, I peer.

I am at High and Over
High, over my head,
Parascenders, sit beneath coloured wings,
Yellow, orange, pink, blue, green, red.
They drift . . . up there
Like an aerial ballet
With each current of air . . .
In pure grace,
The only sound,
The breeze, brushing their face.
That of my beating heart . . .
Enthralled, by the pure beauty
Of this grandiose Sussex part.

Peter W P Turner

Can Believe

Well you've thought, I've won, and fought, true come sending -
Of it all, though it's not, in there begot,
Stands in time, for to, appal.
Why it happened, hear one say, thought that I could drift there -
Stand, did the second time in store, same, come after with deplore.
All of which, in there but thine, the minutes on their upward climb.
Come this way, to what was sought, began in ever sorry taught.
Each is all, or what without, come before, in instant sign
Through it is a mere, but o'er, in its shape, had some restore
Where the saying, of the pall, too big are large, but ever small.
Size, realise, it's all of shape, not that I would know of drape,
Not as if it's there at all, forever tiny, it is so small, speck
Is back, and there come track, search of which it can be where
All of that, to understand, gives of each, it's powerful stand,
Though it's small, quite large and meek, seems it's turned the
other cheek
Its fore but stand, has gained the spectre, of upper hand, for have a
Say, it can my own, compare in day, what thou has shown,
So we reap, and there come store.
Through the spend, of one before,
All but do, for each as lay, go in time, to there come fore,
Where's it all or what's about, I heard you saying, let it come out,
All of which, to call for then have this moment, of the shout.
Tried, denied, or done without, sorry mess, is what in time,
Have with o'er, in midst of day, you can believe you're here to stay.

Hugh Campbell

I Little Thought

I little thought, when I saw the woods
So finely mantled in russet and gold,
That in just a week the frosts would come
And winter's first tale would be told.

I little thought, when autumn's emerald green
Clothed the fields, that in just a week
They would be veiled in purest white,
Buried beneath snows so smooth and sleek.

I little thought, when I saw the grey squirrel
Peeping out from a maze of trunks,
That in just a week they would be frozen over
And look like crowds of shivering drunks.

I little thought, when the rabbit scurried
Into his burrow at my approach,
That he would be the last rabbit I would see;
So soon did winter start to encroach.

I little thought, when Christmas came
And I read anew the Christ-child's story,
That jolly old Santa would soon take His place,
Stealing from Him even the stable's glory.

I little thought, when I scoured the shops
For nativity cards, that a round and jovial face
Would be grinning out at me in every superstore,
With red-nosed reindeer taking the oxen's place.

I little thought, when I saw the happy groups
Of ruddy-cheeked children around the Christmas fire,
That outside, in shop doorways and cardboard boxes,
The frozen lay shivering in the mire.

I little thought, when Easter came round again
With rows of chocolate eggs at our beck and call,
That the Lord Jesus Christ upon the Cross
Had died and risen to save us all.

Robert D Hayward

My Hero

He's tall and big and very strong,
He's there all day and all night long,
He guards me in a frightening storm,
Or when I see a ghostly form.
I'll waken in the dark of night,
And know he's there to make things right,
And when I'm feeling sad and blue,
He's there to help me think things through.
He's not afraid of giants or beasts,
And spiders frighten him the least.
He knows how all things work and why,
I know he'd never tell a lie.
If things at school just don't go right,
Or bullies pick on me and fight,
He's there to help without a frown.
He'll never let things get me down.
As long as he is always near,
I know I'll never have to fear.
Who is my 'Hero' big and tall
My *Dad* of course. *The best of all!*

Sonia Mills

I Am Love

I am the babe of stable born
Cradled in loving arms so warm.
I am the child in my Father's house
Learning and teaching, I am no mouse.
I am His son on the river's bank
The dove flew above me as under I sank.
I am tempted by Satan in the wilderness alone,
If I yield to his visions I could never atone.
I am the teacher of my disciples twelve
Showing the way as the scriptures they delve.
I am the angry young man in the temple
To drive out the hypocrites I will not dissemble.
I am the healer of men blind and lame,
Tax collectors and prostitutes call me by name
I am betrayed by a kiss. Oh! The anguish so great,
Deserted by friends, I must live out my fate.
I am nailed to a tree, where the mental strain
Is no easier to bear than the physical pain.
I am the bearer of all this world's sin,
As I go to my Father, more followers I'll win.
I am alive again, even though I died,
Come out of your locked rooms, there's no need to hide.
I am the bridge to my Father on high,
Follow me all the way and you'll never die.
I am love.

Jennifer Stella Smeed

My Cat Has Lost His Miaow

My cat has lost his miaow
I really don't know how-
I think he may be ill
I tried to give him a pill.
I crushed it up into his food -
It didn't do him any good
It stayed right there inside his dish
(I'd mashed it in his favourite fish)
He always seems to know
And it will never go
Into his mouth and down his throat
It's a thing that really 'gets my goat'.

One day I read a special book
(I think my cat also took a look!)
The book said: Hold his mouth 'this way'
It really is as easy as we say -
His mouth will open 'just like that'
Then pop the pill into the cat.
I held his mouth quite firm and tight
He wriggled and scratched and put up a fight.
He was determined not to swallow the pill.
(Our cat can't miaow, but he has a strong will!)
I have to tell you one more thing -
I've thrown that book into the bin.

Eileen Sugden

Meg

(A Fearless Terrier)

Her ageing eyes of innocence
reveal a deep sincerity,
nowhere can one find evidence
pertaining to hostility
towards humanity's pretence.

The shadows of the years begin
to lengthen and encroach upon
a soul uncompromised by sin,
but silently she journeys on
despite life's unrelenting din.

Such faithfulness will never wane
or sink beneath time's fickle tide,
for her expressive eyes contain
more love than mortals can provide
to ease away intrusive pain.

Her heart of courage is immense
when she endeavours to pursue
a cat or act in self-defence,
and constantly she guides us through
life's darkness with benevolence.

Iaian W Wade

Class And Breeding

Once a man born, of low position
He had to accept life's rules and conditions
He was born into a class, and could not rise
He was there to work, to keep betters supplied.
Now as time rolled on, within our nation
There dawned an era of innovation
The government argued, for what seemed a duration
To outlaw class, and form a one class nation
The higher education, in which all could revel
For all that's required, is the odd 'A' level.
They enter university, with a pen and a pad
A luxury never bestowed, on their mam or dad
They receive a grant, this they've been told
And it's far more cash than they'd get on the dole
They attend the lectures, with brains that can't think
For most of the grant, has been spent on drugs and drink.
They spend much time at the hole in the wall
And in a short time they've spent it all.
They years roll by, and they get their degree
And they say to themselves, well, that'll do me.
They've spent most of their time sitting on their arse
Trying to convince themselves, they are now, middle class.
To them the working class are not worth feeding: - *Now*
Any style can be adopted, but class is in the breeding.

John J Hudson

My Sweet Diamond Ring

My sweet diamond ring was all aglow
On the day he said he loved me so.
But where is it now? I really don't know
I've searched high and I've searched low.

I cannot smile and I cannot sing,
Until I have found that precious ring.
I have turned out cupboards, moved the bed
Even ransacked the old garden shed!

I'm not concerned with the cost of the ring -
Just the symbol of love and everything.
Oh, I do believe I am going to cry;
I will rue this day till the time I die.

No other diamond could be quite the same.
But I have only my careless self to blame.
Wait for one moment - I am sure I can see
That sweet sparkling ring 'smiling' back at me.

Joyce Hemsley

Wishing

Oh, to awaken each day with a smile
To greet the sun as brightly as it greets me
What a wonder that for a while
Life could be bright for you and me

Oh, if only to walk many a mile
Each day in the bright sunshine
Where everyone we met wore a smile

Well, I can dream can't I, for a while

Janet Fish

MAN'S JOURNEY

How different to stroll
Foggy pathways at night
The paths you thought you knew
Have disappeared from sight
Once familiar places
Become displaced again
Can I really be lost?
I ask searching in vain
The ghostly outlines of
The distant dwellings there
Throw out a dismal light
Onto the midnight air
You start to wonder if
The path you're on is right
Then your footsteps slacken
Until you reach a light
Cast from half hid lamp
Suspended up on high
Mounted on a column
It melts into the sky
Skeleton lamps appear
So unexpectedly
In places so strange
In places you cannot see
At last you start to see
A most familiar sight
And then you know for sure
The path you're on is right.

Terry Daley

FACES

If I were to write about the faces I see,
Everyday - everywhere, all around me,
And guess by their look, what's deep down inside,
I am sure I'll find something that would hurt my pride.

Faces of children, innocent and free,
Faces of grown-ups, as sad as could be
Faces old - that reveal sufferings of the past,
Borne with endurance, till the very last.

Do I stretch a hand and say 'How are you?'
Do I ever smile, from sentiments true?
Do I by a word soothing and kind
Try to dispel thoughts that oppress the mind?

And help my poor neighbour to build up some hope
When he is in darkness and does nothing but grope.
Groping for something beyond one's reach -
Oh how much that smile, that handshake, that word could teach.

Do I ever pay back with a good deed,
My neighbour's misgivings - when he is in need?
Except in a mirror my face I can't see -
But I can always tell, what's deep down inside me.

Josephine Pollacco

Mourning Anger

We are all gathered here today,
To remember Dad, who has passed away.
Weather's bad - high winds and rain,
To friends and family - a day of pain.

The vicar staggers, his speech is slurred,
Most of his words, cannot be heard.
A man of the church he's meant to be,
A so-called friend of the family.

The service is short and lacks spunk,
Obvious to all the vicar's drunk.
'Communion wine it's sure to be,'
To me it smells more like whisky!

The Book is shut and he totters out,
No words of comfort to the devout.
Then off he goes at full throttle,
No doubt to get another bottle.

He does not fear the Bishop's wrath,
'Retired' but a disgrace to the cloth.
His only reason for being here,
The funeral fee - to buy more beer.

Douglas Bishop

INCOMPREHENSION

O Lord of all Eternity,
Forgive us our stupidity
When we try to make You fit our human span.
We harness your immensity
And try to grasp infinity
And cannot understand Your boundless plan.

Our often weak humanity
Almost becomes insanity
When we measure You upon our human scale
Your awesomeness and majesty
Your power, might and sovereignty
Makes every thought we have completely fail.

O Lord of endless sympathy
Look down on our iniquity
We want to worship You, O holy one
We come in all humility
And utter inability
Then find you in the person of your Son

For He left Your sublimity
And took on man's depravity
And suffered grief and pain and total loss
But You, O Lord, did raise Him
And for this we'll ever praise Him
For we find You in the wonder of His cross.

Catherine May

Inside Story

I wonder . . .
If I were an insider
To a spider -
if I were a web-winder
I wonder
how I'd be feeling . . .
Web-dreaming
Or suctioned to a ceiling,
walking the wall -
would I be afraid to fall . . .
I wonder,
If I were an insider
to a spider,
if I were eight-gate-legged
with multiple eyes in my head
would I mind
if a careless hand came to unbind
my home:
Would I welcome
the sun
lighting up my strong, fragile thread:
Would I be led
to feel like an insider
would I be a fly or a dream-catcher
Would I be a truth-finder . . .
I wonder
if I were a spider
would the world seem the same place of wonder
it seems to me
through the eyes I see.

Jocelyn McKinnon

BEYOND BELIEF

(On the birth of Ben Lewis Harrison)

As dark turns to light
The moment gets near
Longing for our baby to appear
Through the night he got stronger and stronger
Hoping he won't be much longer
Waiting, and time doesn't seem to pass by
We need him here quickly,
I feel I could die.

All of a sudden, it all becomes a rush
'Everybody' telling me to push
Silence falls all around
He's coming fast! Without a sound
He's here! They shout, as I sigh with relief
Our baby boy, beyond belief.

As I look down at him lying on my tummy
He is creeping up, for a cuddle
He knows I'm his mummy
Warm and soft with rosy cheeks
Blue fingers and eyes
That try to 'peep'
His hair is dark and soft to touch
This new little stranger
Who we love 'so much'.

Lisa Harrison

PACEMAKER

Have a little pacemaker
I call it my dear friend
Expect it here for ever
Until the very end.
When it was time for surgery
The team all around
I was very confident
Boastful, it may sound.
Couldn't be in better hands
As anyone could see;
They would do their very best,
Their very best, for me.
The surgeon and his team
Were full of dedication
I was nothing but
Full of admiration.
What would we do without them
Many wouldn't be here today
Given a new lease of life
How can we ever repay;
So, this little rhyme,
Is just for them you see,
With a great big thank you
For what, they did, for me.

Mollie Catlin

THE VALE OF TEARS

There is a place called 'The Vale of Tears',
filled with loneliness, pain and fears.
Surrounded by people we may be,
yet our Calvary they choose not to see.
Hearts are breaking every day,
yet no one has the time to stay -
to offer kindness, love or support.
'I'm much too busy!' they retort!

So Jesus reaches out His hand,
through His servants, who have found -
that for them, He found the time to stay . . .
'The Vale of Tears',
for them holds no fears.
They learnt that Jesus wept for them.
His love washed the pain out of their hearts,
His Holy Spirit offered a new start!

He lifts up the head bowed down so low,
gives dignity, self-respect and helps us show -
Others trapped in 'The Vale of Tears',
some have been there for years and years!
He gives us courage to help them stand,
bringing to us, and them, fullness of life,
and songs of joy to replace the strife!

Margi Hughes

TRUE FRIENDS

Now in advance we cannot tell
On whom we can depend,
But coping with our loss and grief
We know who are our friends;
For some, so steadfast in good times,
So often let us down,
But one who's there, in our distress,
A true friend we have found.

So many friends just make a call,
Express their sympathy,
To get involved, give of themselves,
They do not want to stay;
About our heartaches and our fears,
They do not want to hear,
So many want to share our joys,
So few to see our tears.

True friends don't ask if they can help,
They come, do all they can;
Don't comfort us with feeble words,
Just hold us in their arms;
Through all our pain and suffering,
While needed, they are there,
We thank our God for all such friends,
For they have proved they care.

G Whitten

The Wings Of Autumn

High on the mountain, sun-baked, green
Wild rosemary scents the autumn air
Dark purple shadows contour the ground
Over snow-white villas dotted around

Below in the distance a silvery sheen
Reflected shadows, on warm currents of air
Dance and flutter in the dusky light
Stars sparkle as day turns to night

Aroused, frantic, swift, mean
The cold north wind buffets the air
Sweeping rain-clouds across mountain tops
On down to the sea, anger spent it stops

Out of reach a golden moonbeam
Caresses the mountain's cool still air
Where the bracken old and gnarled
Clings tight forever free and wild

Sheila Pharo

Starry Night

Are you awake?
Would you like to see?
Are you awake?
Will you come with me?

Come to the window,
We'll draw back the drape,
Look through the window,
Can you make out the shape?

The stars are in place,
In the midnight sky,
Some stars even race,
Whilst we sleep, you and I.

Such wonders to see,
In the sky are portrayed,
Such wonders are free,
In God's heaven displayed.

June Prescott

THE NEW ALLOTMENT

'I have a plot.'
'A plot, for what?
To rob a bank, to write a story
An epic brave and bold?'
'No, I mean a patch.'
'A patch for trousers,
A patch for pain?
Or those that smokers use in vain?'
'No, at last I have a plot of land
I fully mean this earth to till,
I know my back will ache and break
My joints will creak
My hands will never be the same
When Mother Nature stakes her claim.
But I'm inspired to sow and reap
And She will give me all I need.
Just let me plant that precious seed.
I cannot wait, come rain or shine -
So keep away - this plot is *mine.*'

Barbara Delaney

Ye Olde Curiosity Shop

Let us go on a visit to ye olde curiosity shop,
Down the end of the lane, the very last stop.
The tram departs from the village green.
Oh what wonderful sights to be seen.
Jewellery, trinkets, fancy goods and pottery,
Never in my life have I seen such cluttery.

The sign on the door says *'Come in and browse'*,
Such interesting disorder my senses are aroused.
Dolls, teddies and toys of a bygone age,
Marionettes with costumes, their own private stage.
Look around, inspect, please take great care,
And breathe in the atmosphere old fashioned and rare.

But what are we looking for in this curious shop,
Priceless antiques, that will not shock.
Barter, haggle, that is our main aim,
For if the price is right, then it's a bargain.
So pretend only mild interest on our visit, don't stay,
Then leave this Aladdin's cave and be on our way.

Bernice Sharpe

A Pig's Life

'Oink!' went the pig as he took another swig,
Of the swill that lay down by his feet.

'What a way to live!' exclaimed the little pig,
'Where I play is where I sleep *and* where I eat!

What would be the harm,' he asked the man who ran the farm,
'If I moved in with you - in your house?

I would not be any trouble, I'd even shave my stubble,
If you asked I'd be as quiet as a mouse.'

Well the farmer, he said, 'No!' and told the pig to go,
Back where he belonged, to the sty.

So the piggy wandered back, but what worried him was that,
The farmer did not give a reason why.

Well, later on that week, while dreaming in his sleep,
That he was not a piggy but a man.

The farmer's podgy wife got him with her carving knife,
And turned the pig into a joint of ham!

Gordon Knight

WE TALK OF LOVE QUITE OFTEN

We talk of love quite often
From all those younger days
The love we have for siblings
Our parents every day
We fall in love eventually
Then want to spend our life
With someone very special
To be their loving wife
As children add to children
Our love forever grows
With pride we watch
As years go by
And so the story grows
The love we have is endless
Given gladly where we can
When we are blessed with grandchildren
We take them by the hand
The joy returned is endless
This love will spiral, grow
We talk of love quite often
As the years together flow

Jeanette Gaffney

I Want To Be An AA Man

I want to be an AA man
And drive around in vans
With a heavy duty lantern
To hold in both my hands -
A krypton bulb and waterproof
With high performance lens
A fully rubberised finish
With a battery that never ends.

I want to be an AA man
And wear a bright green coat
Reflecting in the headlamps
With my tool kit in the boot
With my siren flashing bright
I'll rescue damsels in distress
I am the fourth emergency -
I'm better than the rest.

I want to be an AA man
But . . . oh dear . . . I'm a woman
So . . . I'll take my new torch and reflector jacket, and keep
Myself safe while I walk the dog on the common!

Jane Phillimore

Dreaming!

I can hear you!
Standing there!
In the hallway, on the stair.
On the landing, down below.
Don't you know! ' I love you so.'

Time is passing, all the while.
'Hey' I'm missing, your sweet smile.
Love is living, by your side,
I know you'll always be my guide.

Telephones ringing, I hear the tone,
When we are talking, I'm not alone.
'Hey' I love you, don't you know.
And my heart will never let you go.

Time's a-ticking, ticking by.
This day I'm ending with a sigh.
Because I'm dreaming, dreaming of you,
And in the darkness we are two,
Happy people, joined as one
And forever, we'll go on!

James Ellis

The Salvation Army Band

The Salvation Army Band was playing
The day that God called me
In the notes I heard 'Rise And Follow Me'
The worshipping music reach up to heaven
And angels sang in tune
So joyful was the Salvation Army Band
On that warm night in June

The Lamb of God lead the parade
Round the Heavenly throne
The marching saints were endless
To that Heavenly tune
I wanted to rise up and join the happy throng
But I knew my work was not done
I said 'Sorry Lord I'm not ready
To give you my hand.
Because Lord I'm a member
Of the great Salvation Army Band.

Freda Lily Lawrence

Cooking For Christmas

Upon a large tarpaulin,
'clomped' flat where cars should turn,
rose a mound as for the fallen
in some war states chose to spurn.

Topsoil, grit and blue-green clay -
a muesli for the worms -
the diggers heaped day by wet day,
light fading at each spade turn.

Scarab-ish, deliberate,
they passed the time blasé -
pausing ever to cough and spit
where the children liked to play.

Pasta-stretching each small task,
kneading the overtime,
leavening pay cheques (need you ask?)
to spend Christmas with a crime.

Perry McDaid

JOYS OF THE KING'S HEAD INN

The Southwold King's Head,
Has a restaurant so fine,
Serving good food,
From seven till nine.
Freshly caught fish,
And great veggie dishes
Steak, chicken and duck,
With chef's succulent sauces.
So begin with a starter,
Finish with a mouth-watering sweet,
A few glasses of wine
And you're in for a treat.
The waitresses are ready,
The chef's set to please,
But Johnny's dad says
'He won't eat peas.'
Young Tim's thrown a tantrum
He's creating a racket,
Auntie Maude can't have chips,
It must be a jacket.
'I'll have the duck,'
Booms the haughty lady in blue,
'And a few sprats for my husband,
Served with salad will do.'
There's a crush at the bar
And nowhere to sit,
An hour's wait for food,
Chef's having a fit,
Waitresses ready to drop,
Kitchen staff round the bend,
Then, suddenly, it's over,
We've coped in the end.

Rosemary Remy

ARROGATUS

I'm a natty looking guy in a suit
The uniform of an office worker.
I fiddle and faddle with paper all day
So that proves I'm not a shirker.

I swan up and down in my company car
A two-litre brand new Rover
And say that I know the Chief Constable
If the boys in blue pull me over.

I spend a lot of time at the golf club
It's a must if you want to go far.
I talk birdies and eagles and so on
And I have my own tab at the bar.

My mistress is a cute little redhead
With exquisite tastes - trés bon!
She used to be my secretary
Till the rest of the office caught on.

Wife? Oh her - she's probably at home
I haven't been back for some time.
The twins? Well, as far as I know . . .
I guess they're doing just fine.

Whadya mean by repossessed?
Of course the mortgage is paid.
Or was I distracted the other month
Entertaining the local barmaid?

Kids in care? How did that happen?
A breakdown - my wife? Is that so?
Well it doesn't surprise me, as last time I went
I thought she'd let herself go.

Jeanette Smith

GINGER TOM CAT

Ginger Tom cat
Safe and dry
Smells wafting -
Apple pie.

Ginger Tom cat
Kicked out in the rain,
Scratched the door
Again and again.

Ginger Tom cat
Sheltering in hedges,
Thinking of fish pie
In humongeous wedges.

Ginger Tom cat
Going insane,
But then he's brought
Back in again.

Ginger Tom cat
Safe and dry,
Smells wafting
Apple pie.

Lucy Porter

THE HOLIDAY HOME

Autumn came fading the summer blue,
stealing the warmth enjoyed by the few.
Creeping over the dunes and bay,
hid in the old house yesterday
Shedding her damp in every room,
peeling the walls, she stood in the gloom.
Chilling the house and bringing the rain,
hungry, the hearth, and longing for flame.
Empty, alone, the holiday home,
harken the wind in the chimney groan.
If only the sound of a human foot,
where everything's tidy and neatly put.
Restless the smuggler hung by the neck,
a legend, the night, of the terrible wreck.
Dangle the rope still tight to his throat,
wander his ghost in a captain's coat.
And who can tell if he comes from hell,
with the flotsam amid the swell.
Alone in the holiday home to stay,
where everything's tidy and put away.
And there to lodge not a soul to care,
until the spring, as long as he dare.
No one today would ever believe,
he'd left the spray, when they found the seaweed.

A E Doney

SNOOKER, OF COURSE!

I've just got a break, no not my leg!
I've just had a slice and it's not bread!
I've had a swerve, not in a car!
I've had a screw and didn't get far!
I've had a cannon and it didn't fire!
I've had a kiss but with no desire!
I've had a rest and not any play!
I was under the cush, tucked away!
I've used a spider, in fact quite plenty!
I've got a double and it wasn't twenty!
I've been up the bulk, yes many a time!
I've had a pot but it was no crime!
I've had a plant and it didn't grow!
I've had a cue but it was on no show!

I suppose you think I'm really crazy
Like a very mad, mad horse!
But come on, use your brains,
I'm talking about snooker now, of course!

Frank Parker

ALL HALLOWS EVE

The night is silent now and still,
The darker thoughts have vanished,
The moonlight touches the far hill,
Nightmares now are banished.

The wind sings in the wilderbrooms,
Where gorse and broom all golden lie,
Songs that rise with gentle tunes,
Red rocks standing closely by.

Outside is quiet saintly peace,
Inside the hush of sleeping,
Dreams full of magic to release,
Until the dawn is peeping.

All Hallows Eve be blessed tonight,
By starlight pathways gleaming,
Everything will turn out alright,
Good times are brightly beaming.

Kathleen Mary Scatchard

The Cold Face Of Winter

Autumn is fast fading from view
Taking with it all shades of hue.
Winter has turned his face around
With him he brings those wintry sounds.
The blustery winds and lashing rain
Playing noisy tunes on your window panes.
The nights are dark, the moon hangs low
And trees their ghostly shadows throw.
Flurries of snow whip across the open fields
And Jack Frost his icy patterns will yield.
Small creatures seek warmth in the earth below
Safe from the ravages of the winter snow.
The robin will come to look for his food
For he understands winter's cold moods.
Nature slows down and seedlings sleep
Deep in the warm earth, safe in its keep.
Until Mother Nature her glories perform
And spring is here, new life is born.

Iris Taylor

LEAVES AND BROKEN BRANCHES

Leaves and broken branches, drift on gutter rain,
mirrored image of mankind, can they feel the pain,
sympathetic glances, as we see them pass,
the end has come, life has gone, left with only wrath.
Where once there was beauty, praised from all the skies,
in things that moved, and ones that stood, pleasing to our eyes,
created in love, in colours to brighten the scene,
is this the end, as they pass by, if the best has been.
Wait! Leaves and broken branches, winds whisk them all away,
flying high, they come to rest to say,
life is not over, tree roots here to feed,
here we'll give new life, to acorns from a seed.

M Burleigh

THE GREATEST LOVE

The female love changes
With each aspect of her life
In childhood, she loves as a daughter
As an adult, she loves as a wife
But when she bears a child
She finds a tender, new emotion -
A protective, sacrificing
And overwhelming devotion
As the family grows
There is always love for more
A mother's loving spreads
Like the sea's ripples on the shore
Her love embraces all her family
Like flowers within a garden wall
If you have grown up in that garden
You have known the greatest love of all.

Una Allan

My Backyard

Out of my kitchen window
I see a place so fine.
The trees that beckon to me
Stretch up to life divine!

My patio is simple
Where we have barbecues.
In summer when it's hot (we hope!)
We have no time for stews!

The grass I see before me
Is verdant, pure and lush.
The flowers grow so cheerily,
A multicoloured crush!

My husband grows the veggies,
Potatoes, beans and such.
He's always working out there,
Sometimes it gets too much!

Just beyond the garden
A peaceful river slides.
To gaze upon this water
Will calm down my insides!

What else! Ah, yes, the guinea-pigs
In hutches made of wood.
They both eat all our lettuce.
I hope it does them good!

Often when I'm working
I gaze upon this scene.
With all these riches close to me,
I feel just like a queen!

Judith Thomas

We Are All Equal

Of different people we make fun,
It isn't the way a society should run.
Boy, girl, disabled, black or white,
We live in a multi-cultural society and this isn't right.

If you're black, then you're a 'nigger',
If you're disabled then we snigger.
If you're a girl you're not very strong,
What is this society doing wrong?

What does it matter if you can't walk or run,
You still breathe the fresh air and feel the warm sun.
Just because a wheelchair is how you get round,
It doesn't mean they have to be house-bound.

When it comes to a job, who do we employ?
A 'paki', a 'cripple', a girl or a boy?
Does it matter who they are,
Everyone has the chance to make it and go far.

You have a job, what more can you say!
You clean the floors and it's rubbish pay.
What else can you expect, you're black!
Now get on with it or you'll get the sack.

This is what some people have to put up with every day,
We should be nice, this isn't the way.
We treat some people like dirt and make them our slaves,
So in this big ocean we call life, let's make some waves.

Colour shouldn't matter to you or me,
It's the person inside that matters you see.
Everyone in this world has the same right,
Boy, girl, disabled, black or white.

Penny Bunce

PHEASANT WEDDING SPREE

Under the cherry tree
my true love said to me
'Pray bide your time
still be free
'tis no season for a wedding spree
'tis the month red chestnuts fall
'tis the month the bugle calls
to the hunt of the master of the hall'

Under the cherry tree
my true love said to me
'Pray give me time
let me be
'tis no season for our wedding chime
'tis the month of the grunting boar
'tis the month of the gun and gore
the tightening noose of the poacher's war'

Under the cherry tree
my true love said to me
'Pray in good time
I'll wed thee
at the season of the shooting corn
at the month of the budding thorn
at the cry of the fawn just born
we'll hail the season of our wedding morn'

Françoise de Pierpont

One Word

There is a word that's often used
In many ways it is abused.
It crops up many times a day
And always in a different way.

For some the word acts like a balm
In others it will cause alarm.
Which way to take this sentiment
And it is really truly meant.

It may be used in merry jest
But the true meaning is the best.
When your world is in turmoil
This one word can make you smile.

Troubles come and troubles go
Someone, somewhere will feel low.
A touch, a whispered word
Already the troubles shared.

The old, the young, the in-between
All know exactly what I mean.
Alas, there are a frightened few
Who'll never take this point of view.

Those of us who wait in vain
To have this word linked with our name.
Silently we stand and weep
And our awful secret we keep.

One word brings hope and joy
Either to a girl or boy.
Young or old we're all the same
To us love is a wondrous name.

M A Honeyman

Splish! Splash! Splosh!

I've tugged my new red wellies on again.
Struggled into my toggle-coat and hooded hat.
Mum's dressed up in her pretty plastic mac.
She says 'It's going to rain -
Not that there's anything new in that!'

So off we go, and sure enough
It buckets down and wets us both.
There's oodles of the soggy stuff.
Mum cries 'Mind that puddle, use your loaf!'
Too late! I'm not one to hesitate so it's -
Splish! Splash! Splosh!
And me? I'm thrilled to bits!

The next big puddle stops me in my tracks,
For, looking down, I see another me - but -
When I kick the puddle once again, I've gone!
'That's funny Mum,' I say, 'how can this be?'

The water stills - I look again
To prove there's no deception.
'Come on,' says Mum, impatiently,
'It's only your reflection!'

Splish, Splash! Splosh!
What fun the rain can be -
Though not much fun for Mum, perhaps,
Just fun for little tykes like me!

Betty E Keeler

HOPE SPRINGS . . .

We haven't heard a single word.
It's been three years of hell.
The last time our Jack wrote to us
He said: 'I'm fit and well.

I'm having a great time here, folks;
This place is really cool.'
He'd taken a year out, you see,
From when he'd finished school.

He'd gone to roam around the world,
He wanted to be free
To find out about life and such
Away from Dad and me.

He'd worked his way round France and Spain.
He'd saved enough to pay
His passage through to India,
But somewhere on the way . . .

Dad says we might not ever know
What happened to our Jack.
But I live with the tiny hope
That one day he'll come back.

The phone rings, and my heart leaps up.
Dad tries not to look grim.
I cross my fingers, though deep down
I know it won't be him.

Jenny Proom

A Mountain Stroll

I walk towards a distant hill
Grass and moss carpet my feet.
I am a lonely traveller
For the hill to newly greet.

Prickly yellow gorse, and slushy bog
Impede my way.
As if to hold me for a while
That I might more survey.

Vivid colours, on shades of green
Where wild flowers, in profusion grow.
Twisting silver streams, in morning sun
To lazy rivers flow.

Bees busily search for 'nectar of the gods'
Winged insects hum their way, on zig-zag course.
Earthbound denizens forage for food
From any source.

Birds wing their way
In the clear air.
My nostrils fill, with a heady scent
Gracious nature, deems to share.

My progress to the hill has stopped
My feelings make me sigh.
What do we miss, when we're in haste
And have a focused eye.

Idwal B Holt

One Day I Looked For Her

What happened to my little girl when one day I looked for her
For there, in her place I found this very bright 'nearly' teenager

Gone was the shy, timid daughter, I knew so well
In came discos, mobiles, CDs, make-up and hair glitter gel

She really has come into her own since starting Grammar school
She oozes self-confidence and everything is now considered 'cool'

But still she loves the Simpson's, and her room is still in a muddle
And we do have lots of giggles and still find time for a big cuddle

So now you know my Emma, perhaps as much as me
She is a pleasure and a bonus in our family

Christine Saunders

With Thanks

My sister is no longer, with us, the undying love of my family,
And all the people who fought to make a miracle.
My sister's arm . . . so small and limp will now be part of me,
As I was once part of her.
This heartfelt gift of undying love.
When I grow up I will know of the skill, that was used
And indeed, mustered by the '55' team of surgeons
And their attentive assistants; who for fifteen hours,
Used their skills and knowledge, their time and devotion, love and care.
This minuscule attachment, so precious a thing, in a myriad of ways.
All creeds and cultures, will work and pray together
For this little twin sister.

Joy Townsley

When Winter Comes

When winter comes
Everything goes away
I heard a robin singing
Somewhere in the trees
I looked but couldn't see him
He was hidden by the leaves
He sang 'Oh so sweetly'
Every note in place so neatly
The rain has stopped falling now
A rainbow can be seen
High above the trees
All the colours of the falling leaves
Slowly floating to the ground

What a lovely time autumn is
All the leaves falling down
Red, yellow, orange, brown
Covering everything around
Soon the trees will be bare
Leaving just the wood there
When the wind blows
Branches fall
Those poor trees left
With nothing at all

J M Drinkhill

A Time For Rhyme

We have had many years without words that rhyme,
So don't you think it is about time,
That those who prefer contemporary lines
Went back to what real poetry was considered in the good old times?

After all the background does come from the old master,
Whilst admiring things that are a little faster,
It would be so nice to know that some do study the works of old.
After all there is so much that is silently told.

Poetry is really only a short story,
Emulating some past glory.
So if you really wish to be grand,
At something simple try your hand.

There are plenty of folk who write words with a twist,
So why make life harder and add to the list?
I've lost count of the times I have heard people say,
'But it's not fun like it was in the good old day!'

When poetry is apt to rhyme,
One can always improvise when they've forgotten a line.
It makes reading and writing verse much more fun,
And laughter abounds from everyone.

Betty Green

Felix

He froze, betrayed by whiskers white.
A shadow in the grass. A sound so slight.
In friendship I approached. The shadow
Unfroze. Became a cat in flight.

Hence I trod the garden path with care.
Casually, feigning to be unaware
Of green eyes narrowed in the sun,
Watchful from the shelter of his lair.

At my outstretched hand he growled disdain.
I wondered - what could be his name?
Hazarding a guess called - Felix?
Impelled by hunger to the plate he came.

My caresses warily rejected,
Each day, once his food accepted,
My housemate, mistrustful yet,
Stalked away with tail erected.

Until the night, leaping the window sill,
Graciously he offered me his kill.
For me the furry life extinguished,
Tapering tail and dainty nose so still.

As I bent towards the lifeless form,
Felix, with unwonted gesture warm
Butted my face, our friendship consummating,
Suspicion and hostility forsworn.

Homeless once, alert to hostile tread,
Curled for warmth, paws protecting head,
Subsisting on an undernourished mouse,
Now lies he in purring slumber on my bed.

Geraldine Page

NIRVANA

Golden sunset, blush of dawn,
Jewel-dewed cobweb, frost on lawn.
Primroses when the spring is nigh,
And deepest blue of midnight sky.
The evening star before the night,
Formation of the duck in flight.
Sweet melody of birds who sing.
Bright colours of the butterfly's wing
Gentle touch of west wind breeze,
Copper bronze of autumn leaves
Snowflakes pattern on cold morn,
Warmth of puppy, newly born.
The valley low and mountain peak,
Waterfall clear stream does seek.
Soft dappled velvet of young fawn,
Red poppy in the yellow corn.
Meadows blessing, woodland lark,
Silver moon to lighten dark.
An azure sea with white-gold sand,
Lace foam as sea caresses land.
Shells a-scatter on seashore . . .

Could Heaven offer any more?

Anita Richards

I Wish I Had A Mummy And Daddy

I wonder what her name is. She comes here every day
I watch her through my window as she and the other children play
And that must be her mummy who she runs to
When each game is through
And gets all those hugs and kisses, oh I wish I had a mummy too

When it's nice they eat a picnic sitting on the grass
They always seem so happy as they wait for the time to pass
Until he walks through the iron park gates
With a lovely smile on his handsome face
Oh I wish I could have a daddy who would take me from this place

He swings her round high into the air and she laughs
And screams out with glee
Then hand in hand they all go home but sadly never ever notice me
The people who care for us in this home keep us clean
And we're well fed
And they make all of us children brush hair and teeth
Before sending us to bed

But they never tell us stories or tuck us in each night
And are never there to comfort us should we wake up in fright
Sometimes I cry myself to sleep as I lie there in the dark
Wishing I had a mummy and daddy like that little girl in the park

Don Woods

Rubbish

Rubbish around
Lots on the ground
What a nuisance you are
If only people put you behind bars

If only people would put you in the bin
It's better for our streets, gardens, it's not a sin
It's up to us how we treat our space
Not seeing it in shifts, now that's ace

Not seeing it makes our streets look good!
If everyone did their bit as you know we should
Then this nuisance needn't be a bug
And government, civilians wouldn't have to grudge

And government, civilians can't blame the fool
Whom they see pushing rubbish with the right tool
Rubbish running on the ground
If we all picked some up, then there won't be much around!

Yvonne Burgess

Autumn

Autumn is coming,
So keep on running,
With the wind blowing,
Autumn is coming.

Leaves are falling,
Trees are bare,
The trees are rare,
Autumn is coming.

The flowers are turning,
The petals are falling,
The storks are appalling,
Autumn is coming.

Kids are running,
Kids are falling,
Kids have the flu,
With the dogs too,

'Oh no!'
Autumn has arrived!

Marie Stewart (12)

FEAR

Inside the darkness I can taste my fear
Unable to move, no voice do I hear
Inside the darkness is an empty abyss
No pleasure to experience, only death do I wish
Inside the darkness no one cares that I cry
I am lost and alone and I wonder why.
Inside the darkness no light filters through
But somewhere recognition that I must start anew.
Inside the darkness I scream and shout
Only my higher self capable of getting me out.
So I listen to my intuition that says start right here
Out of the darkness I begin to appear
I feel uncertain of where I must go.
Out of the darkness a seed of hope must now grow
No one else can do it for me
Out of the darkness I will gradually see
A life full of hope and happiness to share
Out of the darkness I will meet you there.

C A Jones

WHO WANTS TO BE A MILLIONAIRE?

Sixteen thousand pounds
The compere screamed with glee,
The cameras, lights, the people
All looked down at me.

The next one really matters
A grand, or thirty-two
But I don't know the answer
Whatever shall I do?

A, B, C or D
I really could choose any
I'll still go out a winner
I came without a penny.

But what a gamble I would take
If I should choose just one
I may lose fifteen thousand pounds
But it's really been good fun!

Or shall I quit
At this point in time
Give up my chair
To the next in line . . . ?

I think I'd better play it safe
A gambler I am not
I'll take the sixteen thousand now
I'm happy with my lot!

Patricia Anne Turner

CONTEMPLATION AND OBSERVATION

To witness the joys of the Cotswolds
Means excitement and anticipation,
But the eve of departure brings worries,
P'raps sleeplessness and trepidation
Lest alarm does not ring the next morning,
With delays, which would cause consternation.
By the time we reached Moffat for coffee,
We'd to dash, to avoid inundation,
But we drove on to Oxford, no bother,
Though some road closures caused us vexation!
We visited Blenheim, then Rousham,
(On each we were given narration),
And next day we're taken to Batsford,
To see trees of each variation.
Then off in the heat to see Hidcote,
For that was the next destination.
We hurried towards Chipping Campden,
Wilson Garden, a quick visitation,
Next, Garden Botanic of Oxford
Which was just a short ambulation.
Free time was a bonus, to wander,
'Classic Tours' was a pet occupation.
That evening was spent in the 'Old Dining Hall'
Watching slides, in a fine presentation.
On our journey back home, by the east coast this time,
Driver Bill added modification,
Garden centre to see and to browse through the rows
Of more plants, giving yet more temptation!
Such a great time was had on our five days by coach,
We were sorry it reached termination!

Catherine Buchan

STEAM DAYS

Sunday walk . . . no park today,
today, it was the engine shed,
my father took my hand in his,
the fear rose in me, as he led
me under the black and broken roof
the steaming monsters, high above me
in their towering cave.
He lifted me in his strong arms,
I'm trying to be brave.
Marooned high on the footplate,
the gleaming track below,
brass dials and a small iron door
when opened up would show
a glowing hell of sparks and soot.
My father and his fireman cooked
on a polished shovel, eggs and bread
numb hands a simple meal would share
with stinging eyes . . . amid the grime.
Three pounds a week, a steady wage.
A boyhood dream, a bygone age.

Bobbie Dee

MR MOON

Excuse me Mr Moon
but you should be in bed,
it's daytime now you know
and the sun is here instead.
She lights our daytime hours
as you light up the night,
so for now I'll say goodbye
and Mr Moon, sleep tight.

Sue Cox

In Praise Of The Dome

In this country there is a divide,
Have you or have you not been inside
The Millennium Dome?
Have you been influenced by those at home?

When we went it was a bright day,
There ten hours, before coming away.
We were impressed with the site
Indoors or outdoors, such a feeling of light.
Not too crowded, not long to wait.
To explore all the zones, no hassle, that's great.
There were parties of guides and schools from the north,
Couples young and old scurrying back and forth.
Families determined to miss nothing on view,
The staff were friendly and helpful too.
A variety of food, different places to eat,
The only problem - the poor old feet!
So we relaxed and watched the spectacular show,
One hundred and sixty two perform in rotation you know.
Conservation and recycling were a big theme,
Something that must not be just a dream.
I saw hope for the future and care for the past,
Things that were temporary, others that last.
It was good to be near the Thames, in its majesty,
This helped give us a feeling of history.
Our favourite zone? It's hard to choose just one,
Home Planet, Work and the Journey were fun.,
Was it a celebration of time since Christ's birth?
Did you judge for yourself, the Dome and its worth?

Susan Holmquist

Aspects Of Love

Lover of the sea
  Able seamen am I
Wise as wise can be
  When storm winds blow, sigh.

Sounds of waves billowing
  Gaze at myriad stars above
Full moon a'shining
  Image in mind, my own dear love.

Moon on the wane
  Shore leave soon to come
Heart longing again
  For my love, my dearest one.

Sages of old did say
  Sailors (some) into temptation fall
Weak, lonely, astray
  In far port of call.

Love powerful strong emotion
  Be it ever faithful, true
To loved one give trust, devotion
  Happiness, life long, thus sure.

I Lott

THANKS FROM A STRANGER

The stranger entered a west end bar
Produced a five pound note.
'Beer' he cried in a strangled voice
From the bottom of his throat.
The bar man took his money
Then served his pint and change.
The man then gave an awful shock
To everyone in range,
As he took his scarf off
And went to drink his beer,
They saw he had a dreadful scar
Which stretched from ear to ear.
The cockney, leaning on the bar
All he could say was 'Cor
In all my life I've never seen
A wound like that before.
Wherever did you get it mate?'
He said 'The Falklands War'
They said 'This man's a hero
Let's have a quick whip round.'
And in less than no time, two hundred quid was found
He pocketed the money, made a beeline for the door
And as he left he muttered '*Muchas gracias Senior!*'

Norman Chandler

ODE TO BOOZE

The initial lubrication
 Is the supreme titillation
  Which fills the digestive
   System with a sense of satisfaction,
    While the internal fermentation feeds
     Your mind intoxication that leads you
      On a journey to complete immobilisation
       There followed by a sense of pleasant gyration.

With a need of irrigation
 Followed by regurgitation,
  In complete capitulation
   Comes a state of mesmeration
    And of course hallucination and
     With much accumulation, and
      Maximum hydration in complete inebriation
       There is just one compensation:
          Sleep.

Derek J Morgan

HAPPINESS

What is happiness? Happiness is found from within
Do not search, you will never find
Just look to yourself, it is in your own mind
Just sit back and close your eyes
Use your imagination and you will realise
The peace that comes from within
It is a peace beyond price we all can win
So do not search for happiness you will never find
Just sit and meditate
It is there in your own mind.

Glenis Dando

Autumn

Autumn love, autumn beauty
autumn time, autumn duty
to seek the needs of the winters ahead
bless those of no love, give many a bed
pack a gift to a foreign land
let an unknown child have a toy in hand
share with newness the coming of joy
bless every heart to fruitfully employ
the crispness in seasons, Christ's birthday told
dancing angels their praising to *explode*
opening the gates of heaven, His love in endless flow
touching lost souls renewing thy blessed glow
to feel the peace of holiness, His presence so near
shining a light in their darkness, a way now clear
'yes' He is the befriender, the builder, love is His answer
brother and neighbour *He* is our saviour

Linda Daly

The Frost Bird

Frost bird weaving
through the swirling mist
brown crested, wing dappled
ruff snow-kissed
green back shimmering
from the arctic pools
flame lit, tail tip
smouldering up the plough
fiercer beauty echoing
Iceland mirage seen
moments meeting - moments greeting
fuller being - gleaned.

Ancilla Dent

Old Man

There's a spring in your step, old man,
That you've never shown to me.
There's sunshine in your smile, old man,
It warms my heart and stokes my soul.
And when our bodies meet, old man,
Your message is electric!

Have you changed the time, old man,
Or were dreams last night wild and free.
Did lusty youth revisit you, old man,
And leave you full of longing.
Was it something to do with the moon, old man,
That's put stardust in your eyes!

Your sunshine and your spring, old man,
Would you save them awhile for me.
Then a game of wishful thinking, old man,
Together we could play.
I'd not share it with the rest, old man,
Our secrets I would keep!

For the sake of make-believe, old man,
Pretend I woke you from your sleep today,
Sending waves of pleasure through your veins,
That now I burn beneath your skin,
That it's me, old man,
Who's dancing through your mind!

Karen McBean

VOLCANO'S THREAT

Volcano with majestic cone
Sitting quietly on its throne,
Suddenly its anger flair
Erupting far into the air,
Shaking the earth with a mighty force
Spewing lava, makes its course,
Rolling, spluttering spitting fire
Destroying all, that's its desire,
Lava flows with burning fury
No one had seen this augury,
Uprooting, burning, ravaging
The red-hot molten seething
Spreading its fingers far and wide
Obliterating mountain side,
No bush, tree, creature alive
Had any chance to survive,
Boulders black, size immense
Scorching hot their heat intense,
Torching all within their path
Leaving death their aftermath,
No time to run, all perished there
This lovely mountain stripped bare,
All that lived below its feet
Now in cold grey pumice sleep.

J Naylor

BOOK OF DREAMS

Dreams -
Share the playground with sleep,
Where reality and fantasy,
Often together - choose to meet.

Where truth and fiction,
The mind can confuse,
As slumber, remains a pupil,
Unable, to leave the room.

Suddenly, without warning,
- To wake up -
And never know the ending of the adventure
Only to wonder - if - 'what', 'why', and 'but'.

For dreams can never be found in any reference book,
Only invisibly written on pillows,
Where rest as the author with sleep,
In the night's library, choose to look them up.

Bakewell Burt

BEWARE

Beware for your soul and how you treat it,
Beware what you eat and how you eat it,
Beware what you say and how you say it,
Beware what you do and how you play it,
Beware what you think and how you think it,
Beware of your cup for you have to drink it.

We all have our cup that no one can borrow,
For what's in our cup we have to swallow,
To drink of our cup determines our marrow,
Don't let it get filled with sin and with sorrow.
Let God fill your cup with His peaceful hallow
Enriching your soul with hope for tomorrow.

D J Tucker

CARELESS

You were careless
But nevertheless
Couldn't care less
You were fearless
Yet I was careless
Things were priceless
You were cheap and careless
Wild and reckless
Couldn't care less
Anxious and restless
Possessions meaningless
In a world that was careless
I mean you didn't care less
That's right
Careless
Yes I was
Carefully careless

Ann Copland

WEE 'BON'

Her eyes of hazel, her little wet nose,
Her wee soft pads, her sweet little toes,
A chubby wee body, and ears of velvet too,
My darling baby 'Bon', I love you.

So many years go by
And still you're just as sweet
As the day we saved your life
And swept you off your feet,
To live with us in our place called home
No longer do you have to roam.

We love you as you play with your ball,
Roll on your back or sit in the hall.
You really are no trouble to us
To see you happy, gives us a real buzz.

So we thank you little baby 'Bon',
For protecting us and ruining our lawn.
We thank you too that we always make up
After you're naughty - cos you're our little pup.

Julie D Coventry

BLUE MOON?

What is this that I see in the sky?
What is this beauty catching my eye?
As I look to the up through my sunshield of green,
I find that the moon is this image I'm seeing.
This calm pale blue crescent that's lighting my way,
This cool luminescent from so far away.

It draws my attention, it draws me so strong,
It takes my attention as I drive along.
It takes me so wholly that I fail to see,
The wheels of infinity heading for me,
As I ponder of life with a blue moon instead,
Death's chariot hits me and now I am dead.

Richard J Godwin

Prelude To Summertime

The herald of spring is the snowdrop
- As its head gently nods in the breeze
Next comes the croci, a colourful crop
And buds bursting forth on trees.

Primroses in their pale yellow hue
Anenomes scattered in woodland moss.
Bluebells - a carpet to view
Whilst campions their red-heads toss.

Hark! To the gentle drone of the bees,
See frolicking lambs in the meadow,
Birds flitting from tree to tree,
Watched by a sleepy old sheepdog called Shadow.

Pale sun shining in an azure sky
Beckoning summer days' gentle haze,
April showers passing by
Distant sound of seashore waves.

Swirling seagulls circle the sky
- Cometh those long lazy summer days.

Kay House

The Dream

I had a lovely dream one day
  As I sat beside the sea;
A ship was sailing into shore
  With a cargo just for me.

It anchored right beside me,
  And out jumped all the crew,
They showered me with diamonds
  Pearls and emeralds too.

They gave me lovely diamond rings,
  For my fingers, one and all;
And gently round my neck they placed
  A lovely silken shawl.

I did not want to wake up
  From this dream, so real and sweet;
But then I had to let it go
  As the waters reached my feet.

I jumped up quickly on the sand,
  I could hear the sailor's call,
And round my neck still floated
  A lovely silken shawl.

Marie Wilson

TIME'S UP

After supper they sat down by the fire,
Then - 'I'd like to present you with a clock,' he said,
'I recognise the time you've spent on family.
But now the kids are fully grown, left home,
Where I ask myself, does that leave you and me?'

Rising quickly, he offered her a box,
'I appreciate the work that you have done,' he said,
'I like the comfort and the service you provide,
But man cannot live on bread alone, when all's done
And the love I had for you has long since died.'

He held her hand and looked her in the eye.
'A friend of mine has bought this house,' he said,
'I'll provide you with a comfortable annuity,
I've purchased you a flat, and that's that,
I guarantee you'll always have security.'

He left her side and headed for the door,
'I hope that we can still be friends,' he said,
'I'm leaving now for one that I desire,
Time passes, seconds tick, our lives are through so quick,
And you're no longer quite what I require.'

Joan Burdon

God Is In Every Poem I Write

I feel a power, a presence, surging over me
It stimulates my brain, my heart, my hand
It commands me to write about the things I see
I think about God's creation - and I understand

And as I put pen to paper, words come flowing
From the windmills of my mind
All God's beauty lies before me, and inspirations I find
The sun and sky, the trees, the earth
The stars at night, the waning moon
The dawn gently breaking, the singing birds so full of mirth
The dewdrop on a rose, on a summer's morn
A little lamb just newly born

A sunny day, the joy it brings,
The church steeple, the bell that rings,
Familiar faces of children, full of laughter
Each new day, and the evening after
Bringing hope and peace to all mankind
All these things in God I find
He is in every poem that I write
His presence felt, but out of sight

Mary Seddon

POETRY

I have a soft spot for the old,
For stories that in rhyme are told,
This, I was taught is poetry,
And rhyme and rhythm were great for me.

Pick the things that you want to say,
Write, rearrange, find a rhyme, okay,
Then find a rhythm and feel the flow,
Anyone can be a poet you know.

Exams aren't important, those you don't need,
Just let your mind free to sow the seed,
Whatever the troubles or joys in your head,
No one to tell, but consider it said.

Spoken our loud could almost be song,
That's not to say any other is wrong,
I'm well aware that it isn't a crime,
If all of our poetry doesn't rhyme.

All the great poets who wrote from the heart,
Would hate to know it's a disappearing art,
So, for me, until the end of time,
A poem should be made to rhyme.

A T Giddings

HALLOWE'EN

The ghosts and ghouls have come out to play,
on the 31st of October - Hallowe'en, their special day.
Witches, demons and vampires unite,
to frighten people worldwide, all through the night.
The sky is black,
the clouds are grey,
good Christian folk, stay away.
The wind howls violently,
the trees vigorously shake,
the skeletons rattle in the graveyard,
ready to be awake.
Children, all around, are playing trick or treat,
eager to be asleep, before evil gathers top meet.
A big desolate mansion, stands forlornly upon the green,
with bloodthirsty apparitions revelling around it,
the most horrendous sight ever seen.
The floorboards creak,
the footsteps on the staircase pound heavily,
into the dark, mournful sitting room,
the Satanists dance about merrily.
Pumpkins are lit, the mighty cauldrons bubble,
spells and potions emerge, for an evening of deadly trouble.
Black cats are everywhere,
to take centre stage today,
their eyes full of deadly malice,
for anyone who gets in their way.
I lie in my bed finally and I tremble with dreadful fear,
as the approach of the Hallowe'en underworld, draws ever so near.

Fine Buliciri

Cat-Thief

He really is quite a cat!
Worth seventy-five grand for all that.
Turkish angoras are fairly rare
And this one's stud fee's beyond compare.
Just under a year ago
New owners bought him to show
Him off at cat fairs contentedly
And with it pick up a handsome fee.
But how he's theirs no more.
How the German cat-thief swore,
Dark glasses and scarf obscured her head,
When the owner confronted her and said:
'Give him back! He belongs to me!'
The thief legged it athletically.
She ran to the green Peugeot getaway car
Which by now has conveyed the angora cat far
From his lawful Lowestoft yard.
The police now are on their guard.
At airports around the continent
To see if they somehow can prevent
The smuggling to Germany
Of a cat which should really be
With the Collins' family in Lowestoft.
From under their nose he was whirled aloft
And spirited away.
Oh how they regret that day!
Gone is Antonio B Ricardan
The prize cat who surely had élan!

Julia Middleton

TICKING AWAY

Seconds tick by, seasons fall,
What's it like not to care,
Not to care at all?
If the moon will rise,
If the sun won't set,
What's it like not to care
If it does or forgets?

Rivers run dry; floods, they fall,
What's it like not to mind,
Not to mind at all?
If everything's lost
And faith it falls down,
What's it like not to mind
That we've crashed to the ground?

Cuts turn to scars, the scars remain,
What's it like not to care
If they do or they fade?
If the wound's left open
And never to heal,
What's it like not to care
If the pain's fake or real?

Lives tick by, generations fall,
But why should you care,
Why at all?
If the moon won't rise,
But the sun has set,
Will it only be then
That you form some regrets?

Kate Stobart

A Walk On The Moors Above Haworth

High on the moors this bright summer's morning,
watching the wind turn the heather to sea,
wild waves of fantasy billow around me,
enchanting my heart and setting it free.

Onward I wander, lost in my reverie,
through shades of amethyst, amber and green.
High in the heavens, a lark, singing solo,
is cushioned on harmony from murmuring stream.

But dark clouds are gathering on the horizon.
Passion and tragedy brood in these skies.
Poignantly held in a sister's embrace,
I'm viewing the scene as through Emily's eyes . . .

Created and nurtured by her loving hand,
(her story conceived in the wind and the rain)
Cathy and Heathcliff are formed from the shadows.
Genius is born out of heartache and pain.

I willingly drown in this dangerous love,
carried away with tumultuous bliss.
Their names ride the wind as they welcome their destiny.
There never has been a love stronger than this . . .

A soft gentle breeze clears the veil from my eyes.
Sweet on my face now, the sun, warm and kind.
The glory of nature, her desolate beauty
is bringing a comforting peace to my mind.

Echoes of yesterday sigh in these grasses,
hopes for tomorrow soar on the wing.
Time and again, I'll return to this hillside,
this magical place where my soul learned to sing.

Ellie Lomas

FAT CAT

There once was a man who had a cat.
He fed it till it grew so fat.
He used to stroke it with a broom.
And when it purred it
shook the room.

Eating, eating it could not stop.
Growing, growing till it went pop.
Then one day a dog it saw,
he then went up to shake his paw.
The dog just gave a frightful pant
he thought it was an ele-phant.

Bridget Drinkwater

THE DREAM CATCHER

You catch all dreams
Within your web,

Allowing only the
Good to fall to my head.

The others you hold
Until the light of day

Where the rays of the
Sun fade them away

So each night when the
Dreams come to play

A dream catcher will
Keep the horrors at bay.

Sally Bush

The Cure

He came home from work full of snuffles and groans,
And sneeze followed sneeze without warning,
So I tucked him in bed, ignoring his moans,
Saying 'See how you feel in the morning.'

He stirred about nine and I took him some tea.
I thought he was looking much brighter,
But men never grow up, I'm sure you'll agree,
And I knew how to deal with this blighter!

'Send for the doctor, I'm going to die'
He moaned from his bed, feeling sicker.
'If you're sure you're really at death's door' said I,
'I'd better call round for the vicar.'

'No, no, please don't leave me, I'm failing quite fast.
I may not survive many hours.'
'Well if you're quite certain you're not goin' to last,
I'll order the funeral flowers.'

'You're heartless and cruel. My mouth is quite dry.'
He croaked in pretended distress.
'There's water beside you. I'm going' said I
'Into town for a nice new black dress.'

'Suppose when you've gone that the Grim Reaper comes?'
He whispered with awesome self-pity.
'I'll bet that you'll soon be the closest of chums.'
I replied, thinking that was quite witty!

He started to grin. 'You're a hard one.' he said
'My future's decidedly gloomy.
Okay, so it's only a cold in the head.
I ought to have known you'd see through me!'

Patricia Farley

Burning Passion

How good to have a bonfire and see the smoke rise high
Get rid of garden rubbish when it's gathered up and dry,
But in this year two thousand it simply isn't done,
You must not cause a nuisance by blocking out the sun.
We used to burn our refuse many years ago,
Before the ozone problem had begun to show.
Fires were rich and glorious with flames that leapt and sparked
Neighbours slammed their windows and Rex and Fido barked.
To do the deed on Monday grievously offended,
Sheets were snatched from washing lines before the smuts descended.

Like a chain of beacons were summer's funeral pyres
All around the country competing with the spires,
While the pungent smell of burning wood
Was incense for the ritual mood.
We must conserve our planet so the experts say
Recycling of everything is the accepted way.
So weeds and twigs must all be stuffed into plastic sacks
And then transported to the tip in spite of aching backs.
A queue of cars and trailers is blocking up the road
For conscientious gardeners are waiting to unload.
Conservation we are learning, though some are far from keen
We must refrain from burning to keep the country green.

Rosemary Cook

RETIRED

Why is it assumed, that when you retire from work and strife,
That you now have simply nothing to do, you have retired from life,
But no, no, no that just isn't true, because you rapidly find,
You have so many new strings to your bow, and of the enjoyable kind.
You don't have to go out when it's raining, when skies are
cloudy and grey,
That's the time you get down to reading those books, you've
collected along the way.
You can take off whenever you want, to places far, far away,
Or you can leisurely amble out, to the seaside or country each day.
But maybe sometimes you'll wake up, not feeling too well or bright,
So that's the time to just take it easy, you can't always be
flying your kite.
Then of course you may fall prone to illness, sometimes fall by the way,
But medicine now is making swift strides, they are finding
new cures every day.
Never, never stop learning, there's such joy in discovering new things,
It can be very surprising what you're capable of, go on,
stretch your wings,
The wings of your imagination, try new ideas and such,
Then you'll find my dear friends, that you are enjoying
retirement so much.

Eileen Cuddy-Buckley

TELL ME WHY?

A little child crept into church one day,
Quietly she went to the altar to pray.
'Sweet Jesus, can you tell me why
You've taken Granny to the bright blue sky?

Daddy told me she was suffering pain
But now she's with you she's better again.
If you've made her well I'm very glad,
But I do miss her, and feel rather sad.

I know you love Granny, I love her too,
She was always telling me stories of you.
Dear Jesus - Daddy's been crying today
As it was his mummy you took away.

So Jesus please help my daddy to know
That you are with us wherever we go.
Please tell Granny that I do love her still,
So does my daddy, and we always will.

Oh dearest Jesus both of us love you,
And though you took Granny, you love us too,
One day I know that my daddy and me
Will see Granny again when we live with thee.

Now sweet Jesus I'd just like to say
I feel better for talking to you today.
I'll go and tell Daddy that when we are old
We'll meet you and Granny in your loving fold.

Oh, dear Jesus, I forgot to tell you,
I will love and serve you my whole life through.
Tell Granny I'll try not to cry again,
I know she's happy in your heavenly plane.'

N Young

THE NAIL-SCARRED INVITATION

Come, ye heavy laden, in your weariness,
Come unto me, said the Lord, and I will give you rest;
Take my yoke upon you, and in turn learn of me,
As in spirit and heart I am meek and lowly,
And your souls shall find solace - a restful delight,
For my yoke is easy, and my burden is light.

And the spirit and the bride unite to say 'Come,'
Urging every hearer to give due attention,
For this glorious invitation is yet offered still,
And is available to the 'whosoever will',
Promised to one and all who, searching, are thirsty -
The pure water of life, to take and drink of freely.

Yes, to the life-giving waters come without delay,
And come just as you are, though lacking means to pay,
To buy for your deepest need, without money, without price,
For salvation is freely offered in Jesus Christ;
And the bread of life is to the needy soul food,
So taste now and see that the Lord is indeed good.

And, as His grace extends to the far ends of the earth
Through the Saviour who came to bring the second birth,
Why then will you perish, and God's provision refuse?
When naught on earth can compare with the gospel's good news
Of one who gave His very life-blood to win our salvation,
And whose loving hands now us beckon in nail-scarred invitation.

Ian Caughey

CRUNCH TIME

There's a mint in my coat pocket,
That I'd really like to eat.
It's sort of green in colour,
And would just go down a treat.

It's one of those that's crunchy,
And full of gooey stuff,
But I can't eat my sweetie,
'Cause it's covered in some fluff.

I really should have thought of that,
The day I dropped it in.
That pocket's always fluffy,
And the mints came in a tin.

I suppose I could de-fluff it,
But some bits are truly stuck.
If I could find some tweezers,
They'd all come off with a pluck.

Hang on though, why not buy some more?
They're really not that dear,
And mints do lose their taste if
Left in pockets for a year!

Steven Millhouse

OVER MY DEAD BODY

The graveyard was quiet and everything was still,
When Charlie suddenly remembered his will.
He had left it upstairs in an old biscuit tin,
Which when they cleared up, would be thrown in the bin.
He pushed on his coffin lid, to try and get out,
For he knew from where he lay, it would be useless to shout.
His coffin lid lifted, and his ghost stirred that night,
As he looked around there was no one in sight.
He went to his old house, that he knew so well,
To find someone there that he could just tell.
He heard voices shouting, as he drifted through the doors,
Charlie said 'That's mine' and 'This can't be yours.'
They were all far too busy as he drifted up the stairs,
Shouting at each other 'That's for me,' and 'This is Clair's.'
He took his will out of the tin, then lit it with a match,
He slipped out through the window, and pushed it in the thatch.
The flames spread quickly, his relations ran out in line,
'My spirit will never rest in peace, if they get what was mine.;
When I had life, not one of them cared, even when I was ill,
So now I've made quite sure that they get nothing in my will.
He then lay back in his coffin, and closed the lid down tight.
His spirit was quite peaceful now, and he knew what he'd
done was right.

Nita Garlinge

Residuum

Not of course what I expected,
would at one time have rejected,
the bright of heart, the light of heart.

But one must learn
one cannot choose,
cannot choose what one will lose.

Hold fast, cling
to the bright gold ring.

What heart dreamed would follow
leaves as fleet as the swallow
in search of the spring.

Where now is the ring,
the bright shinning ring?
I am left with the hollow, the hollow.

Louise Rogers

A Verse Too Far

Some modern poetry goes too far.
Can leave you wondering where you are,
with metaphoric hills to climb.
Though what it doesn't do
is rhyme!

E J Nickson

My Quiet Place

The green of the grass meets the blue of the sky
Shimmering river runs close by
I see each peak of the hills beyond
A dragonfly lands on a wavering frond
Leaves are whispering in the trees
Gently swaying in the summer breeze
A skylark is singing overhead
As kingfisher swoops to river bed
Clouds are drifting silently past
Anglers' line and bait are cast
Quietness and calm is everywhere
Pervading through the country air
The time has come for me to depart
I leave it all with a heavy heart
As I pack to wend my way home
Once more this scene my eyes do roam.

Marion Pollitt

You

You are the sunshine in my sky
The apple of my eye
You are my umbrella in the rain
Medicine when I'm in pain
You have arms to hold me
When the world turns me away
You have the key
To unlock my deepest mysteries
You are the sunshine in my sky
The apple of my eye.

Colin Farquhar

Behind The Scene

Adored by all her loyal fans, she was their one and only.
Yet with all her beauty and her talent, she was very, very lonely.

She was just an ordinary woman until fame came on the scene.
Used and abused by all and sundry, when she hit the silver screen.

When you are rich and famous, adoration is a must.
But when it comes to friends and lovers, who are you to trust?

Somehow you are merchandise, something just to sell,
But living in the spotlight, can be a living hell.

They love the parts that you portray, villain, lover, hero.
Yet underneath the fantasy the real you is down to zero.

T A Napper

Loss

One flower droops in crystal vase
Fading like the last bit of light.
A ray of sunlight plays on copper.
Briefly the room appears bright.

This room where she did her dreaming.
This room where we shared our thoughts.
This room where children played and,
Her gentle wisdom sought.

No more shared thoughts in this room
No reflecting on our hopes and fears.
An unfamiliar quiet surrounds me - must leave
Before the flood of held-back tears.

Betty M Varley

THE GHOST OF DREAMS

Through fields of green I walk alone
Where once you walked alone with me
I sit where once we sat when first
We both agreed to disagree
Since we've gone our separate ways
I seldom see you anymore
So now I sit and dream where once
We shared our dreams in days of yore
What seemed unfair in retrospect
Was bound to come to pass, because
How fragile was the bond we shared
And frail the love that never was
The times our paths have crossed since then
Are few and far between, although
So many times you haunt those dreams
That we once shared so long ago
So once again, though now alone
To linger 'mid familiar sounds
And ponder feelings long suppressed
I walk again these hallowed grounds
Where, I expect, it's best confront
What is, when all is said and done
The reason why I question what
Has drawn be back three decades on
For I suspect, what must be, is
And realise it's for the best
To face the demons at their worst
And lay the ghost of dreams to rest.

Pat Fortune

ODE TO BLACK BEAUTY

You stomped along our garden path with such a forceful tread,
Facing the world so boldly, you didn't bow your head.
But as the days turned into weeks, still you were seen to roam,
And it became apparent that you hadn't got a home.

Now we loved dogs, we'd known no cats, they didn't us enthral,
In fact our lifestyle wasn't geared to animals at all.
We hoped that some kind person would make a pet of you,
Meanwhile we saved you all our scraps, the least that we could do.

Then came the day you stumbled past in abject misery,
Your eyes, past caring, seemed to say 'Nobody can help me',
A twisted paw, boils on your head, cat flu at its height,
Your unkempt fur in matted balls, your back a sorry sight.

Those stark bare patches sickened us, you had to have your chance.
We couldn't be like those who passed without a backward glance.
We called you our Black Beauty, on you we showered our praise,
Though all your hurt and anguish, our love could not erase.

And so our care continued - and then to our surprise,
A real Black Beauty did emerge, with loving, trusting eyes.
With fur so soft and fluffy, a glossy, bushy tail,
Plump padded paws, not seared and worn on lonely wandering trail.

So you became our 'Blackie', to be with us your aim,
Likewise, to you we hastened home, no need to call your name.
You'd really taken over, no ploy could we resist,
Indeed we'd only one regret - your kitten days we'd missed.

But after six bright, happy years, you then became unwell,
We nursed you through the winter, your age you couldn't tell.
But now your time was running out, our hopes and prayers in vain,
Despite our care, you'd never bask in summer's sun again.

Now as I tend your little grave I visit every day,
The memories we cherish will never fade away.

Doreen E Roberts

River Spey

Mighty is the river fed from mountain streams,
Swirling waters sparkle as on it sunlight gleams,
Endless tumbling torrents, rushing on their way,
Ever on its journey, the magic that is Spey.

The scent of purple heather is carried on the breeze,
Soft winds now of summer whisper through the trees,
Ferns dance where grasses grow again on leafy banks,
Tall pines guard the waters in proud majestic ranks.

Gliding now and winding alongside pastures green,
How beautiful the picture, a countryside serene,
Grey peaks in the distance stand in frowning glory,
Watching over legends and ancient untold story.

Soft the autumn colours as summer glory fades,
Chilly now the river meandering past the glades,
The hint of winter's coming clouds the evening sky,
Snow-flecked is the river where fallen leaves now lie.

Alister H Thomson

Five-Fifteen

A time to die,
The five-fifteen,
A blatant lie,
A lie unseen,
For the cross of hope,
The cross that bleeds,
Soaks the rope
 That hangs from trees.

It's time to sleep,
The child is still,
A dream so deep,
A childless will,
Do not cry,
To him, he true
As asleep you lie
 He will guide you.

Marc Tyler

A Stay In Hospital

A stay in hospital,
We sometimes must share,
At times it's a cross
We all must bare,
Pain and suffering, laughter and tears,
That's the cross we share
And all be aware,
Kindly nurses running around
Their love and caring
Can always be found,
A gentle word, a loving touch,
A nurse's work is worth so much.

Sue Vince

RHYME IS YOURS AND MINE

Every day of our lives,
The things around us will change.
To speak or hear another language,
To everyone it sounds strange.

You don't say hello,
When you mean goodbye.
Do you laugh when sad,
Or over the moon when you cry.

Our actions, our words,
Our meanings, our life.
Changing the ground rules,
Can only bring strife.

Our poetry is a song,
Spoken in rhythm and rhyme.
To neglect these facts,
Poetry is lost, what a crime.

There are places for improvement,
But don't fall into a trap.
Shakespeare or Beethoven transformed,
Into reggae or a rap.

So let technology advance,
Move forward with time.
But our words in verse,
Sound better in rhyme.

A J Ferguson

JASON

Jason was born on the eleventh of May.
The sun was shining, it was a beautiful day.
His mother Michelle was filled with great joy,
She'd just given birth to a special boy.

As I held Jason close, tears ran down my face,
And my mind wandered back to another place.
My first child Anthony was born the same day,
But four days later God's angel took him away.

For thirty-six years the pain lingered on,
But holding Jason in my arms I realised it had gone.
The feelings I had are hard to describe,
It felt like Jason was Anthony, he'd come back alive.

Jason is six months old now and I'm over the moon
I hope he'll be calling me Nanny soon.
To his parents Michelle and Terry I'd just like to say,
Thank you for having Jason on the eleventh of May.

Christina Carville

OLD FAITHFUL

He did not ask a lot from life
He was faithful to the end
A comfort when I felt alone
A true and noble friend

He did not moan about the world
Or of the people in it
Life to him was full of fun
Each day, each hour, each minute

Now he is gone, the house is quiet
What would I give to see
That funny face, that happy look
The joy when he greeted me

Who is this I speak of?
Would you say the description fits
A brother, father, son or friend?
No - just a little dog called Fritz

Bill Williamson

Meg

Meg you are
A faithful star
A gentle comfort
Near and far
Meg you hold
A loyal gold
A ray of hope
When tears unfold
Meg you keep
Devotion deep
In silken softness
Where you sleep
Meg you light
A lonely night
You are the beauty
Shining bright

Rebecca Punter

Abortion

Alone in the room, awaiting results of her test,
Anything you may need, is here on request.
You're three and a half months' pregnant, I'm sure you are pleased,
As she sat there shocked, about nappies he teased.
Holding back the tears, thinking of her lover,
A married man with three kids, he didn't need another,
Clutching at her stomach, she walked an extra mile,
Wondering should she tell him now, or wait a little while.

Inside her womb, a heartbeat could be heard,
In time, the baby, to grow would soon be learned.
'I'm getting bigger now, oh my mammy will be proud,'
Now seeing and hearing, and trying to shout out loud.
'I hope you like little girls, cos Mammy, that's what you've got
I know I'm still very small, the size of a little dot.
I promise I'll be perfect, just you wait and see,
I can't wait to see you Mammy, can you wait to see me?'

'Why did you kill me Mammy?' asked an angel from heaven above,
'Was there something wrong with me, was I unable to love,
Or was it that you had no time, your own life had to come first?
You took your doctor's weapons, and it was my life that you burst,
Maybe Mammy, you'll realise, you made a big mistake,
And find forgiveness within yourself, caused by your lover's sake
I hope you think of me, and I hope that you confess,
Cos even if you love me none, the love for you I bless.'

Mary Hoey

FOETUS

I saw your feet today, foetus,
And being just a few weeks old
Still, I heard some words between us
Across the vast expanse of Heaven's fold.

I'm sorry I've not named you yet
But I think you'll tell me soon.
I wonder if you will forget,
When you arrive into our noisy room.

You are so small and yet so strong,
Defeating all to reach this place.
With angels now where you belong,
They will protect you till I see your face.

I could not believe your neatness
And marvelled at the world I'd found.
I sense wisdom in you foetus,
There's more to you than merely ultrasound.

I saw your feet today, foetus,
Curling toes just ten weeks old
And thanking then, He who made us,
I wept for His Son's feet,
The feet His Mother kissed . . .
Her grief,
When pierced with nails so cold.

L K Clements

Time For A Rhyme

Start them early and start them on time
But most of all with a nursery rhyme
And little Bo Peep and all those lost sheep
How many tarts did the Knave of Hearts keep?

Listen to the story and please take your time
There's so much pleasure when done to rhyme
Children's stories from the good old days
Are read by mothers in so many ways

Tired children with a nursery rhyme book
Will listen to the story then stop and look
A picture of an elf all grumpy and hairy
Or maybe another of a beautiful fairy

But what happens now it's nearly bedtime
And it really would be a terrible crime
As into your bed or cot your climb
We didn't end with a nursery rhyme.

Stanley Swann

Pebbles On A Beach

As the tide recedes and ebbs away
Shiny pebbles remain in their glossy array
They glint in the open sunshine's aspect
Reminders of ancient history from Atlantis to Aztec
A piece of driftwood floats like a wooden raft
Tossing freely on the ocean wave's path.

R Humphrey

If I Have To Wait

I really get wound up, if I have to wait
I can't understand why some are constantly late
My life has always been governed by watching the time
I suppose it's just a bad habit of mine

I've been arriving at work the same time for so long
That if I am late, they know something is wrong
I tend to be early for an appointment or date
To keep someone waiting, I really would hate

Public transport these days is really no go
You can wait ages for the bus, and still it doesn't show
At the railway station they announce trouble on the line
But then British Rail is renown for not being on time

At the airport traffic controllers are on strike yet again
Six hour delays for all flights to Spain
The road is closed for more roadworks ahead
With all this waiting, I've now got a bad head

At the doctor's surgery time passes so slow
My appointment was for half an hour ago
I start to fidget, I cannot sit still
By the time I see the doctor I really feel ill

A night out with a friend, she's always been loyal
But I know she'll be late, it will make my blood boil
I'll go to the pub and order my glass of wine
Sit back and relax, hopefully not noticing the time

Linda Brown

ABANDONMENT

There are so many things I always missed
My mother's loving embrace and her gentle kiss
Thro my unloved years and those suffering heartbreaks
To be cast aside like rubbish upon a stagnant lake

My mother's discarded me, how could I show my trust
All my childhood love and desires were swept away like dust
I was always filled with envy that burned deep in my heart
Thro my long emptiness that was quickly tearing me apart

This anger that filled me had become my awesome breaking load
There I was always fighting and struggling along life's empty road
To who I could show my love when there was no happiness.
Hatred was eating away my heart and my mind echoed my sadness.

My disenchantment and my loneliness became my only friends
I only wanted love, I only wanted my abandonment to end.
The world tells me to face life, why should I stand alone
When deep resentment and the seeds of mistrust have been sown.

Then years later I learn my mother had her children taken away
My deep sadness covered me like her shroud on her burial day
My grandparents blame this brave woman, they said she was to blame
Thro' those hard years of despair and poverty and this is her name.

J F Grainger

BEDDGELERT

The Welsh legend of a dog named Gelert began one sad day,
when his master left home, to go hunting, as was his way,
every morning both dog and master, would leave their home,
to search for prey for food, through the forests they roam,
one day, the hunter hunted alone, as Gelert refused to go,
his master gone, the dog watched over a baby, remaining so,
the hunter's son, resting in a cradle, since the early morn,
all day, the hunter was seeking prey, to feed his newborn,
as the fading sun was finally bringing this day to a close,
the hunter, with fresh food, now returned, to face eternal woes,
back home, to his horror, he saw the cradle bloodied and empty,
and the exhausted dog, all covered in blood, for all to see,
a shocking thought of his dog killing his beloved son, abhorred,
enraged, now the hunter drew his sword, and Gelert was no more,
weeping the loss of his only son, the sad hunter then heard,
sounds that were like the cries of a child, or was it a bird?
Looking behind the cradle, the hunter saw his son, safe and well,
who was on the floor, by the body of a wolf, who lay where it fell,
a fierce struggle had earlier took place, with a wolf and Gelert,
the dog fought to safeguard the child, who had remained unhurt,
now the faithful dog lies at peace in Bedgelert, northwest Wales,
this Caenarvonshire story is now legend, one of many Welsh tales.

Christopher Higgins

THE STEAM TRAIN

Walking along the country lane
We heard the whistle's call
And we glimpsed the rounded puffs of smoke
As they breasted the farmhouse wall.

Youngsters all and fleet of foot
We sped to the railway track,
Childishly anxious not to miss
The swirling smoke from the stack.

We floundered and tripped and fell up the steps
Of the bridge which straddled the rail
Just in time for us all to confront
The Monster of the Vale.

The engine coughed as it took the bridge
And heaved such a terrible sigh
That the smoke rose up and enveloped us
And the smuts in our eyes made us cry.

But smutty, smoky, smeared, content,
We bounced on the bridge in delight;
For one gasping, hurtling second in time
We had shared in the Monster's flight.

Pauletta Edwards

A JUDGE

A judge stood alone, at the Pearly Gates,
St Peter watched, biding his time.
This method on earth, this wee judge had used,
On people not guilty of crime.

'Why are you here?' asked St Peter,
'You surely don't wish to come in!
Whilst scheming on earth, you sought not the truth,
Nor the difference twixt honour and sin.

The law you plied, your wiles to suit,
Your minions worked in fear,
The chancer of the Chancery,
They'd whisper, with a sneer.

So sadly, for you, oft your judgements were wrong,
Your ego meant more than the truth,
And many an honest and innocent soul,
Had their character stained without proof.

So, now you will pay for your arrogant style,
For vengeance is mine, quoth the Lord!
Eternity means you'll have time to repent,
As hell is your lasting reward.'

Fatty R

THE SHIRE HORSE COURAGE

Up and away through the village they go
Stacked with the finest of courage.
The inn is awaiting - not far away
To top up and unload the barrels.

Horses are tied as deliveries are done -
It's down to the cellar to stock.
Then wagon a-ho and out in the sun
'Tis many a time we'll be back.

Locals are drinking, sharing a joke,
Ne'er do they think of the work.
The brew goes down well - or so we do hope
The shire wagon's covered in muck!

'A hi and a ho' and a merry to and fro
Back and a forth to the Inn.
''Tis greetings dear landlord - I offer thee brew
'Twill ready 'em up for a sing.'

Laddies and lasses do dance a gay jig
Full to the brim with the stuff.
Laughing and flirting - greedy as pigs,
A glass to tha lips and a puff.

The music a-takes 'em to twirl in the hay
All buxom young wenches and lads,
Nothing will stop 'em the brew is okay,
To a riotous, rowdy applause.

Thanks to the shire wagon coming their way
To keepeth all joyous and glad.
A clipety-clop, loud riotous neigh,
'Tis time we be hitting the sack.

Wendy Watkin

THE CLOCK

It stands there rarely silent,
Its language is tick tock,
The best of friends we are you see,
But sometimes I could knock
That humble piece of mechanism
Down upon the floor
When it rings loud, then says to me
'You can't sleep anymore.'

The hands of time keep moving on
Right throughout the day,
Travelling round in circles
As the hours just tick away.
It matters not if you're at work
Or enjoying a great feast,
Just like the tide, it does not wait
For any man or beast.

With certainty it rules our lives
At home, or work or play,
It's often that it calls on us
To go without delay.
It has so many faces
To count would be in vain,
Whilst trying to keep up with time
Some people go insane.

The time we're born, the time we die
Is written in a book,
Even food, put in the oven,
Is timed how long to cook.
Everything in life is run
By just two words, tick tock,
I'm writing now with pen in hand
Yes, one eye on the clock.

Phil Robinson

Rose Of Beauty

See the roses clinging against the wall
All in full bloom as if ready for a ball
So formal and so grand in their glorious array
How they brighten up a very gloomy day

Yellow is the one to remind us of spring
Red is of the red breast flying on the wing
White rose for purity when we were yet first born
The black rose springs to mind of death so forlorn

All these fine blooms creating a display
The cream rose reminding those of their wedding day
While the pink rose sets such a colourful scene
With the woman reminiscing of the time she was sixteen

All these shades of beauty before our very eyes
Leaves us to wonder what before us lies
By just gazing at this glorious array
On this wonderful summer's day

Susan Amphlett

To Rhyme Or Not To Rhyme

There's poetry and poetry
Some rhymes and some does not.
Some sticks in the mind like the daffodils,
The rest are soon forgot.

Some are easy to understand,
Some need some help for good measure.
Give me the ones I learned at school,
I still recall them with pleasure.

Pauline Anderson

SONG OF HAPPINESS

A stream gurgles merrily
As it gently flows along
Dear wild bird greets each new day
Trilling freedom's happy song
Wind whistles a haunting tune
Playing tricks as we pass by
Have you not a little song
To replace that mournful sigh?
Sing your song of happiness
Sing it joyously today
For life is far too short friend
To keep romance locked away
Smiles will dance upon your lips
And bright sparkle in your eyes
So please sing your happy song
And let drop that sad disguise
Sing now melodiously
The sweet message it conveys
It may reach some lonely souls
And help fill their empty days
Perhaps a cherished love song
Binding sweethearts though apart
Or melody a band played
As love waltzed away your heart
Croon soft that sweet lullaby
That recalls a babe's pink charms
Or that soaring rhapsody
That took wing in loved one's arms
Sing your song of happiness
Let its magic fill your day
Then you will feel joyfulness
Chasing fast those blues away

Violet M Corlett

SEASHORE SHELLS

Evocative words, memories from my childhood
Which transport me once more to a beach with its tide
When I recall so dearly those sun-drenched days
Spent with my family and friends by the seaside.

On a Sunday school outing or on holiday
By coach or train we would travel with smiling face
To my favourite resort named - Barry Island
Not a proper island, but still a special place.

O! Why could we not live there forever, I wished
How wonderful it would be, playing by the sea
Building sandcastles, hunting for crabs in the pools
Searching the beach for pretty shells, others and me.

Early days paddling, later swimming in the sea
Chasing the waves to be borne back to the shore
With early rubber rings, much later with air-beds
We would spend glorious hours and wish for more.

Then picnics on the beach, plenty to eat and drink
Perhaps ice-cream or candyfloss, then off to the fair
Trying the stalls with darts, rings or target shooting
To win a prize that looked enticing, if you dare.

Speeding down the Water Chute, the Hall Of Mirrors
Riding the Carousel on brightly painted horses
Shaken up, but enjoying rides on the Dodgems
Seeing not believing the Wall Of Death courses.

Then for a fright we would ride the Ghost Train
Where skeletons popped up, with sounds of screaming pain
The flashing machines gobbled up your pennies
If you did win sometimes it was soon lost again.

So memories of castles, shells, buckets and spades
Sand, swimming costumes, funny hats, postcards, the sea
Conjure up for me, a golden time in my youth
When life was so wonderful, happy and carefree.

Terry Daley

Praise Your Maker

Open your eyes and you will see
The wonders that God can provide
He made the birds in 'yon' tree
And he made you and me
And he took all that in his stride

He did it in six days
He deserves nowt but praise
Single-handed our God did it all
He even made folk able
To destroy the tower of Babel
And demolish Jericho's wall

The human machine
Is the most complex there's been
Individually moulded - I mean
There's no assembly line -
- Made a personality like mine
It's all down to God - He's divine

Anthony Gibson

First Winter

Long dark nights,
Snow falling white.

Frost on the ground,
Glistening all around.

Dawn's fragile sun,
Lightens the night air.

Trees standing still,
Branches all bare.

Excited children laugh and call,
Who will make the biggest snowball.

Igloos, snowmen, all things fun,
Will disappear with the early sun.

Time to stop, we've been told,
Snow's all slush and it is cold.

Tingling toes, wringing wet wellies,
Tired children, hungry bellies.

Chestnuts roasting, fire glowing,
Farewell winter, spring is coming.

Nicola Staniland

SEBASTIAN

There lies a young boy in the streets of
saddened heartache.
His eyes were cold and his skin
was as pale as the moon.
He slowly closed his eyes knowing
his heart was waiting to break.
He fell asleep inside a lonely dream,
a dream that was gone too soon.

He was laid to rest by his mother's side
next to the sand and sea.
Where the angels would come to
carry him off into the night.
There he will fly among the stars,
let his soul become free.
In the early rising of the morning sun,
it is his heart that shines so bright.

Lyndsey Louise Watson

AUTUMN JOURNEY

Even though the skies were softly grey,
The gold of autumn spread beside our way.
Yet the cold wind that chilled us yesterday -
- Had faded to a gentler, warmer breeze -
- Which teased the golden yellow of the leaves
To tremble like pale coins upon the trees -
- Where some still lingered in the soft warm air.
Thanks filled my heart that I was travelling there!

Molly Rodgers

THE CHOIR

Wide-eyed and wondrous they stand in a row,
Their shining heads brushed and their faces aglow.
They rustle their papers and shuffle their feet
And finger their cotters, new-starched and neat.

One tentative cough: can he make the high notes?
One half-controlled giggle; they put on their coats.
Eight little angels trip shyly along
For today is the day for their heavenly song.

Eight angels' voices are lifted on high,
Eight angels' faces, a star in each eye.
Eight pictures of innocence, eight little boys.
Eight little singers with one lovely voice.

Then after the service how changed is the scene:
Eight shining angels they newly did seem.
Now they run shouting, it is a stampede
Of eight little monsters, loud-voiced and knock-kneed.

Nina Havers

MESSAGES

A pigeon on a telegraph wire,
Sitting sadly, way up high,
To be a singer was his desire
As little brown lark in the sky.

But singing he could never do,
His dream fell deep in the mire,
A pigeon can only coo, coo, coo,
Whie sitting on a telegraph wire.

His dreams raced into fiction
Wonderful skills *he* would acquire,
Then he had an inspiration
While sitting on a telegraph wire.

As a carrier pigeon *he'd* be a star,
From flying miles he would never tire,
Taking messages both near and far,
Always waving to the telegraph wire.

P Ludgate

THE SEA LOCH

The sea loch, burnished silver by the sun,
Smells salt between stern hills on either side,
Whose rugged moss-clad outcrops, green and dun,
Contemplate the slowly turning tide

And trawlers, chugging back and forth, as they
Take trippers out in search of whale and seal;
No longer used for fishing, but for play,
They'd rather have a purpose that was real.

As once they did, before the fishing died,
But now their crewmen sail them just for leisure,
Recalling long-gone days they sailed with pride.
'Of course, it's work,' they shrug, without much pleasure . . .

I wonder if the sea loch and the hills
Regret such changes as the sailors do?
Perhaps they, too, are biding time until
The fish return and trawling starts anew.

Colin Wright

TRAINS GET MY VOTE

One hears an awful lot about
The disastrous state of the trains
'Caused by shortage of finances'
The railway network boss explains
Such bad service is all their fault
Railtrack does this, red-faced, admit
But it is poor old 'Joe Public'
Who always cops the brunt of it
Nevertheless I love to ride,
Window seat, on all types of trains
For horseback makes my rear end pain
I get earache on aeroplanes
Whether going by bus or coach
Or commuting by motor car
Constant traffic jams and hold ups
Try my patience a bit too far
Bad accident, off power bike
Riding pillion - ended so sore
Was ambulanced to hospital
I won't go on one any more
Too scared to try hot air balloon
And get seasick on ship or boat
So, in spite of reputation
Rail travelling still gets my vote

Tina Lipman

QUESTION

How is it?
That when I'm prim and neat,
Sat upon a parlour seat -
Folk and friends to greet.
No one calls.

How is it?
On days to business I must go
My fingers itch to do that chore.
Then when I'm free -
That chore's a bore.

How is it? When -
The sky is blue, the wind is high -
The laundry basket's empty.
Yet come the rain -
The washing's there aplenty.

How is it?
The cake I plan -
For visitors - turns out a flop.
Yet one I just throw in the tin -
Is beautiful.
I cannot win.

Marnie Connley

JUST ANOTHER DAY

How do you cope
When the nights become cold?
Your cardboard gets soggy and sags.
What do you do
When your fingers turn blue,
Put on a carrier bag?
Where do you go
When you're feeling low and
There isn't a spare doorway to spare?
How do you feel
When your toes start to peel,
You haven't a comb for your hair?
As the wind becomes icy,
Food is too pricey,
Do you dream?
Do you hope?
Do you care?
When the rain's pouring down,
Take a sip from a can,
Wonder if living is fair?
Could you give us a clue,
How to help you?

Janice L Williams

Beneath The Desert Sun

They halted as the crimson sun fell in the western sky,
Concealed the still hot trucks from enemy's eagle eye,
Brewed up, removing sand from noses, ears and mouth,
Cursing the broken, rocky terrain to the south.
Then, leaning on warm metal, drank their tea,
Hot, brackish, sickly with condensed milk, but free
At last to clear throats parched and dry.
Thinking of home and wondering why
They found themselves in this vast sandy waste,
Munching dry biscuits with their sawdust taste.
Silence fell as the red orb slid below the desert's edge.
Darkness swooped down, giving to them a pledge
Of safety until dawn. Huddled in greatcoats for the sudden cold,
They dozed until at first light, 'Stand to!' they were told.
Clutching their rifles, scanned the land around,
At sunrise not a sign of life was found.
The sand, now cool beneath their feet,
Would soon be shimmering mirages of heat.
They mounted, recommenced their dusty, grinding course,
Praying no predatory plane would spy their force,
Longing already for the cool, dark night,
To shelter them and keep them out of sight.

Peter Hicks

LEO THE LION

My name is Leo, and I am a lion;
I'm the king of the jungle, which you can rely on!
I've a tawny body, with a tufted tail,
My shaggy dark-brown mane proves I'm a male.

My home these days is Africa, in open bush or rocky land;
Once I lived also in Asia, from whence it seems I'm now banned!
I'm mainly a nocturnal cat living in a pride,
Resting in the shade by day, hunting nightly far and wide.

A large carnivorous beast am I, killing animals for my game;
But before you humans criticise, remember that you do the same!
I guard and feed my mate and cubs; they are my family.
Never disturb us, leave us in peace, or I'll respond ferociously!

Now you know all about me, Leo, the king of them all.
Grant your respect, don't destroy me; there's room for us *both* to walk tall!
God created this world for all creatures, no matter great or small,
Whether human, animal, whatever; the world belongs to us all!

Christopher Head

REINCARNATION

I'd think I'd like to be a cat;
To be well fed but not too fat.
My masters must be cultured, wealthy
And, of course, extremely healthy.

Cooking and eating the finest of fare,
With titbits for me, so tasty and rare.
I'd dream about my ill-spent youth;
Few would know the real truth.

Of my howling and prowling,
Of my chasing and wooing
The beauteous females
With long, lustrous tails.

I would like to feel that my seed
Would continue my fine breed
For generations to come.
Wise, proud and so handsome.

Like me!

Helen Persse

FRIENDSHIP

Tread gently and softly my friend going by,
For whenever I need you, I know you are nigh.
To help and advise me along life's road,
Always at hand to help lighten my load.

Many years we have travelled along life's way,
Together in unison, happy at work or play.
To laugh at our troubles and share our woes,
To make more friends and perhaps a few foes.

I value true friendship more than financial gain,
For what happiness can money bring after heavy rain,
Like the kindness and comfort you give to me,
Which flows on continuously like the sea.

May we always share this friendship true,
And may our skies be forever blue,
Without much cloud to darken our ways,
So together, we can spend many happy days.

Mary Antcliffe

LIFE TODAY

Why is this life so full of stress
I should not worry, I try by best
The cost of living is so high
It's hard these days to just get by
It seems the world has just gone mad
There is so much evil, so much bad
In the papers all laid bare
So many people just don't care
Perhaps if we could get on track
We could get our feelings back
Have empathy for those in need
Then maybe we could sew a seed
Stamp out violence and crime
Turn the water into wine
To make the world a happy place
And be proud of the human race

S A Clough

FROGGY!

If I will be your Froggy,
Will you be my Lily Pad?
If so I know,
You will make me feel
So glad!
Because in the great
Mill Pond of life,
One thing at least
I can see is true.
Happiness is me and you!
Sincerely,
Love Froggy!

Graham Mitchell

To Elizabeth On The Loss Of Her Pony

Of course, dear Elizabeth,
You were sad to be there,
Your suffering pony's anguish to share,
Her pain is over,
Yours, you have to bear,
You gave your heart
To a pony to tear.

Forget the bad, remember the good,
The perfumed ride through the bluebell wood,
The galloping 'flights' over moor and heath
The dancing hooves cutting sward beneath,
The leisurely hack on a summer's day
By river bank or through field of hay.
The jumps over furze, the jumps over heather,
The sweet smell of horse sweat, the squeak of leather -
The clip, clop, clep in a winter's dawn
On the tarmac road on a frosty morn,
The nuzzling nose for apple in pocket
The stable door closing, bolt into socket,
The sound of her munching the corn from her bin,
The welcoming whinny, the velvety skin -
The love and the trust, right up to the end,
From your loving, beloved, four-legged friend.

All these things are good
And you must be aware
Your Flo was most thankful, to know *you* were there.
There must be a pony heaven, Somewhere.

Jane Finlayson

MY GARDEN GAY

My garden gay, a dream today,
Tomorrow will be true,
A little house, a shady tree,
The scented border's hue.

A chequered path winds through the flowers,
A tiny path for two,
It leads by pretty leafy bowers
Where I often walk with you.

I'll tell you how I still adore,
In autumn as in spring,
And when we walk the russet floor,
A fuller heart I'll bring.

Sweet romance too, our garden sees,
Patricia in her pride,
We glimpse her dress amid the trees,
Her sweetheart by her side.

My heart is now my garden gay,
It does not lack its flowers,
For I can dream whilst I'm away,
Of all our golden hours.

The rose will vanish in a night,
The birds will cease to sing,
But my heart is ever light,
For love's a lovely thing.

Richard Styles

COUNTRY CONCERTO

Opening chords, stillness, silence, calm
Peace, quietness, nature's healing balm
Blackbirds, nightingales singing
Meadows pulsating, hedgerows humming

Whispering grass, skylarks singing
Trees sighing, twittering birds on wires whining
Busy bees buzzing, cheeky crickets clicking
Nightly owls tu-whit tu-whooing

Crowing cocks, cackling hens
Grunting pigs in creaking pens
Miaowing kittens, yapping pups
From the pond quacking ducks

Hissing geese, gobbling turkeys
Croaking frogs and toads
Neighing, clopping horses
Pulling heavy loads

Lowing cattle, bleating sheep
Bellowing bull disturbing sleep
Screaming seagulls diving, soaring
Undisturbed by tractors roaring

Doves from rooftops gently cooing
Crows in tall tree tops noisily cawing
Long-eared rabbits in the corn squeaking
Little harvest mice through fields rustling

Church bells ringing
Choir boys singing
Muffled toll of single bell
Every year of life to tell

K G Johnson

BABIES

There's something about a baby,
That makes me want my own.
Could it be the face of innocence
One will not let alone?

A baby's so pure,
A baby's so sweet,
Although it doesn't say much,
It just sleeps and eats.

A baby can know
If you are up or down.
A smile on its face
Will change that frown around!

A baby becomes a child,
A child becomes teen,
But not even that
Is gonna shatter my dream!

A baby will love you,
As you show it love.
It must be because
It's a gift from above.

And as you grow old,
Your teen becomes adult,
To love and to care for you
As you did it no fault.

Julie Sennitt

INFORMATION

We hope you have enjoyed reading this book - and that you will continue to enjoy it in the coming years.

If you like reading and writing poetry drop us a line, or give us a call, and we'll send you a free information pack.

Write to :-